Music in Early Childhood

Music in Early Childhood is an accessible and practical handbook, which introduces theories and pedagogical approaches for early childhood music education from birth to 8 years and explains their practical application.

Understanding the theories and philosophies behind music education and how these translate into practice is the key to being an effective music educator with young children. This book provides a comprehensive overview of these theories and philosophies. Organised in an easy-to-read format that summarises each approach and theory, the book clearly maps out how these theories are applied in present-day practice. Also included are a wide range of helpful practical examples and activity ideas based on the work of expert educators. This book aims:

- to inform educators of theories and philosophies of learning and teaching in music education for young children and what they look like in practice.
- to inform educators of the history and breadth of music education methods, and how they relate to the present.
- to help educators develop a theory-informed conception of music education that enables them to make informed decisions about the design and direction of their practice.

This book is an essential resource for all early childhood music educators, experienced or just starting out, who want to develop their practice in working with young children as effectively as possible. It will promote an enquiring, reflective and imaginative approach to practice.

Susan Young is former senior lecturer in the school of education, University of Exeter, and Roehampton University, London. She has researched and published widely in the field of early childhood music education.

"In this scholarly, theoretically focused and immensely practical book Susan Young has succeeded in creating what I believe will be a seminal text for all music educators who are developing their praxis with young children. Despite the rapid developments in the practice of music education for the young child over the last three decades, stimulated in no small part by Susan herself, there has been a yawning gap in accessible texts which set out clearly the underpinning theory and philosophy that is essential to ensure critical and reflective music practice. This book fills that gap beautifully and powerfully. Susan has carefully selected, evaluated and curated a collection of the key theories and philosophies which have underpinned music education practice over time, and made a critical case for their relevance to contemporary early childhood music education. This book provides a new and original vehicle to inform and deepen the delicate of art of effective music education praxis. I believe any music educator who engages with this book will be inspired and motivated to reflect more critically on their current practice and take action to ensure it is both empowering and theoretically executed for the young children at the centre of their music making."
Professor Chris Pascal, *OBE, Director, Centre for Research in Early Childhood, UK*

"At last! A bespoke theoretical handbook to guide and support early childhood music practice and research. Susan Young carefully lays out the landscape for us from evolutionary theory to quite specific early childhood music practices and pedagogical approaches. The concise, systematic writing makes this an accessible and essential book for students of early childhood music education. It would be of interest to those studying music education more broadly, for music education and community music researchers, therapists, practitioners and parents/caregivers of young children."
Dr Jessica Pitt, *Lecturer, Music Education, Royal College of Music; Research-Director, Magic Acorns*

"Susan Young provides an incredibly broad overview of approaches to Early Years Education, from traditional, well-established music-centred 'methods' and child centred approaches to the fields of sociology, musicology and psychology. Young encourages us to think critically and practically about how we can apply such thinking in our own work today and signposts many useful avenues of further development which will appeal to both newcomers and more experienced practitioners alike."
Jimmy Rotheram, *Music Lead (Feversham Primary Academy), Advisor (DfE, Benedetti Foundation), Ambassador (Varkey Foundation)*

Music in Early Childhood
Exploring the Theories, Philosophies and Practices

Susan Young

LONDON AND NEW YORK

Designed cover image: © Getty Images

First published 2024
by Routledge
4 Park Square, Milton Park, Abingdon, Oxon OX14 4RN

and by Routledge
605 Third Avenue, New York, NY 10158

Routledge is an imprint of the Taylor & Francis Group, an informa business

© 2024 Susan Young

The right of Susan Young to be identified as authors of this work has been asserted in accordance with sections 77 and 78 of the Copyright, Designs and Patents Act 1988.

All rights reserved. No part of this book may be reprinted or reproduced or utilised in any form or by any electronic, mechanical, or other means, now known or hereafter invented, including photocopying and recording, or in any information storage or retrieval system, without permission in writing from the publishers.

Trademark notice: Product or corporate names may be trademarks or registered trademarks, and are used only for identification and explanation without intent to infringe.

British Library Cataloguing-in-Publication Data
A catalogue record for this book is available from the British Library

Library of Congress Cataloging-in-Publication Data
Names: Young, Susan, 1951- author.
Title: Music in early childhood : exploring the theories, philosophies and practices / Susan Young.
Description: Abingdon, Oxon ; New York, NY : Routledge, 2023. | Includes bibliographical references and index. |
Identifiers: LCCN 2023011913 (print) | LCCN 2023011914 (ebook) | ISBN 9781032362960 (hardback) | ISBN 9781032362977 (paperback) | ISBN 9781003331193 (ebook)
Subjects: LCSH: Music--Instruction and study. | School music--Instruction and study. | Early childhood education.
Classification: LCC MT1 .Y658 2023 (print) | LCC MT1 (ebook) | DDC 780.71--dc23/eng/20230314
LC record available at https://lccn.loc.gov/2023011913
LC ebook record available at https://lccn.loc.gov/2023011914

ISBN: 978-1-032-36296-0 (hbk)
ISBN: 978-1-032-36297-7 (pbk)
ISBN: 978-1-003-33119-3 (ebk)

DOI: 10.4324/9781003331193

Typeset in Optima
by Taylor & Francis Books

For my grandchildren – Ted and Charlie, Alice and Harry

Contents

Preface	ix
Introduction: Learning and Pedagogies	1
PART I	15
1 Musical Learning as Recapitulation	17
2 Behaviourism: Learning through Imitation and Reinforcement	22
PART II	27
3 Friedrich Froebel: Learning through Play	29
4 John Dewey: Learning through Experience	38
5 Maria Montessori: An Environment for Guided Learning	46
6 Susan Isaacs: Freedom to Express	55
PART III	61
7 Émile Jaques-Dalcroze: Learning through Rhythmic Movement	63
8 Carl Orff: The Unity of Dance, Music and Language	72
9 Zoltán Kodály: Singing to Develop Musicianship	81
PART IV	93
10 Jean Piaget: Children's Ways of Understanding	95

11 Lev Vygotsky: Learning in Social Contexts   106
12 Jerome Bruner: Processes of Learning   116

PART V   129

13 Loris Malaguzzi and Reggio Emilia   131
14 Listening and Exploring Sound   139
15 Communicative Musicality   149
16 Music Play and Playful Pedagogies   157
17 Addressing Diversity   168

   Index   179

Preface

Over the last thirty or more years, early childhood music has progressed and expanded rapidly into a myriad of practices. More small children receive more music education provided by experienced, skilful, imaginative and above all enthusiastic and empathetic music educators.

But what I have also noticed is that theory and philosophy have not been interwoven with these expanding practices to create a useful praxis for established and emerging practitioners alike. So this book aims to provide an accessible and thorough introduction to theories and philosophies of music education for young children and to show how they are enacted in practice. My aim is that this introduction will provide a firm foundation from which educators can make their own decisions in reflecting on and developing their practice.

As I wrote this book I held in mind all the early childhood practitioners and music educators with whom I have had the privilege to work as they study for qualifications in early childhood music. I recall their hard work and commitment, their musicality, their laughter and their warmth, and I never tire of learning from their experiences and insights.

Introduction
Learning and Pedagogies

Making music with young children is busy and demanding work – yet also very rewarding. Remembering the words of the songs, managing the equipment and organising groups of small children, perhaps with their parents too, are all part of making the music happen. And at the same time as juggling these many demands, early childhood music educators are continually watching, listening and making in-the-moment decisions and adjustments. Successful teaching combines skilful practical action with thinking in action, about action. Thinking in action requires the ability to make good judgements, on the spot. And the ability to judge well is based on a secure understanding of the range of options and possibilities for practice and their underpinning aims and purposes.

The aim of this book is to support music educators in reflecting on their practice and making those good judgements. It focuses on core questions. How do children learn in music? What do we want them to learn and how? What do we do as educators to enable them to learn? To address those questions we need to look at what philosophers and theorists have proposed about good practice in music education. This book gathers them together, explaining their core philosophies, theories and principles. They are presented side by side so that similarities and differences between them start to emerge. At the same time, it stays close to the real world of young children and music by providing descriptions of how the theory or philosophy is enacted in practice.

A professional early childhood music educator understands that a good teacher is constantly evaluating and modifying their practice. They are not slaves to one method or approach. They are pedagogical pluralists, nomads, using their professional judgement to make choices. They retain a healthy, intellectual scepticism towards the taken-for-granted, new trends or quick fixes. They are grounded and realistic, yet also imaginative, wise and optimistic.

The pedagogical approaches I introduce in this book have been developed by generations of teachers, philosophers and researchers stretching back into the twentieth century and reaching across countries. Ideas about practice have accumulated, newer ideas mapping onto existing. They never stay still. Yet music educators of the past, and the methods and learning theories they developed still have much to teach us. There is a danger that constantly moving forward with new ideas can crowd out the legacy of the past on which contemporary music education has been built. Understanding the past informs the present.

The Need for Theory

Theory and philosophy can seem remote from the down-to-earth reality of practice – or even unnecessary. The 'what' of music education can take precedence: what songs, what activities, what resources. Yet everyone who works in music with young children is working to their own personal theory. They hold an image of children as learners, an image of their role and how they should act out that role. Every educator has a conception of music and what it is to learn music and what success in their work looks and sounds like. Every educator comes away from some sessions feeling buoyant and thinking 'yes, that went well', and at other times feeling deflated. That judgement of 'what went well' is grounded on their personal philosophy and theory of practice. Yet this personal theory is often deep-seated and remains unexamined. To become an effective teacher it is essential to become consciously aware of the premises which guide decision-making: the purpose of music, what music is, what we think children should learn and how. Furthermore these premises need to be always re-evaluated in light of the children (and parents) sitting before us and the current contexts in which we work.

Some theories and methods that I include in this book are specific to music education, internal as it were. This will include the best known approaches, usually referred to by the names of their originators as Orff, Kodály and Dalcroze, and some of the more recent approaches that I introduce in the later sections of the book. They are subject-centred, starting with music. They embody conceptions of music and what it is to be musical. They set out clearly what children should learn in music, how they learn most effectively and how teachers might enable that learning.

Other theories are external. They are philosophies and pedagogies from early childhood education or theories from psychology that have then been interpreted in the work of music educators. What these philosophies and theories have in common is a broad interest in children's learning processes and in designing educational approaches based on those understandings. In this respect they start not with the content, the subject matter of music but with a focus on children and how they learn. In the sections that present external theories and pedagogical approaches I go on to include the work of one or more music educators who have adopted that theory or approach in their work. This brings to our attention some experienced, skilled and insightful music educators: Satis Coleman, Eunice Bailey, Ann Driver, Eunice Boardman, Frances Aronoff, Barbara Andress, Marjorie Glynne-Jones and more. A strong motive in writing this book was to bring to light the work of music educators whose work is less well known or has been forgotten. What is valuable is that these were practising teachers who wrote about their first-hand experiences, so they offer real-world descriptions of practice. There was a generation of music educators, notably from the 1950s onwards who endeavoured to apply theories, mainly from psychology, in practice and their detailed attention to the processes of teaching and learning deserve, I think, to be better known. The dominance of 'the methods', particularly of Dalcroze and Kodály, overshadows the pedagogical innovations of other historical figures whose work could enrich and extend understandings of practice.

Educational Purpose

Early childhood music provision has expanded considerably in the last 20 to 30 years and there has been valuable overlap and influence from the fields of music therapy, community music, performance and entertainment events and general early childhood education. All these different fields have enriched practice and their integration is one of the strengths of early childhood music. However it is also important to be clear on music education purposes because they can be easily elbowed out by other purposes. Another aim for this book, therefore, is to re-balance and bring *educational* purpose into the centre of the picture. Let me explain why I think that is important.

Children are hearing music and being musical in their everyday lives, in their families, at home and out-and-about, probably more so than ever before given that new technologies interweave music into all kinds of media. So from babyhood, young children are always learning in the sense of absorbing and being enculturated into music. Gert Biesta, an educational philosopher points out that what is central to education is not learning *per se* – because young children are learning all the time – but teaching (Biesta, 2013). Teaching is a specific process that happens in experiences that are intended to be educational. I may need to reassure some readers at this point that I do not have in mind a narrow conception of teaching that centres a controlling teacher, fixed curriculum and passive children. A broad conception of teaching embraces a wide range of processes designed to foster learning and to be responsive to children. Moreover teaching is about more than knowledge and skills, it includes positive emotional and social gains as well as intellectual. The term 'pedagogue' is a useful term for a conception of an educational role that is generous, expansive and responsive. But there is no verb from pedagogue for 'doing pedagogy'. So when reading this book I ask you to stay with and think about the term teaching and to consider the processes it involves.

I realise that for many who offer early childhood music the concepts of education accompanied by ideas of teaching and learning are associated with schools, with older children and with images of a kind of formal, rigid practice they want to avoid. Since the majority of early childhood music work does not take place in schools, is designed for very young children, babies even, and is informal and playful this avoidance is understandable. Early childhood music 'people' often describe what they do as leading, facilitating, workshopping, being an animateur or simply as running classes or sessions. But without the term teaching – or educating is another term that might sit more comfortably with some readers – it is difficult to get deeper into the actions the adults take and why. This is the crux of the issue, in my opinion. You will notice, incidentally, that I use both terms, educator and teacher, interchangeably throughout the book. I do this to keep the terminology more open and flexible. I also frequently use the term pedagogy.

An educational music for all children that includes the processes of teaching, or educating, or 'doing pedagogy', then brings essential questions to the fore. What do we do, as adults, and why? What do want all children to gain and how? These are core questions of purpose that also reveal underlying values. Some music educators suggest that right from the start music education should be concerned with training the basic musical skills such as to keep a steady beat, perform rhythms and to sing in tune. Others have stressed that music education should release children's imagination for music and develop their own, inborn musicality and creativity. Alternatively, because music is essentially a form of communication, many blend early music education with language acquisition. Some music educators in the past, as we will see in later chapters, have suggested that music education should instil in children an appreciation of 'high art music'. That purpose might be queried today. Purposes shift with the current social, cultural and political context. What we want children to learn in music, how and why are not easy or straightforward questions. But because they are challenging, they are often sidestepped or poorly thought through. Without a clearly defined purpose rooted in values and principles, music education can be hijacked by those whose purpose is politically strong, as with, for example, the current emphasis on music imparting non-musical benefits such as improvements in other curriculum areas. Or it can be hi-jacked by economic priorities; what sells to parents or what will be attractive to funders, rather than what is in the best interests of the children. Let me stress, however, that this book will not provide ready-made answers, it aims to describe and explain the *possibilities* for practice.

Reasons for Music

Looking back through the years music educators have offered many reasons for why music is important in the education of young children. Some of the reasons lie in music's *intrinsic* qualities. Some of the reasons are *extrinsic* to music. Music can easily become the handmaiden to other areas of the curriculum and other aspects of children's development. In spite of arguments and assertions over many years as to the importance of music in education, little progress has been made and music continues to be marginal to the core curriculum. All too often when music does gain a foothold, it would seem that it is on the basis of its extrinsic benefits rather than its intrinsic value as a unique form of artistic experience. In our current educational climate, the benefits of music to other areas of learning seem to have the strongest persuasive power. So it is unsurprising that many fall back on promoting music in education by emphasising these wider benefits.

However, if music is merely seen as an enabler of other forms of development, rather than for its intrinsic qualities, it can easily become distorted. If taught for its intrinsic qualities, valued as such and all efforts given to teaching music as an artistic subject – teaching music musically – then any other gains will follow as a matter of course, and almost certainly more effectively than if those extrinsic purposes had been the focus from the start. What's more, positive outcomes cannot be guaranteed by just any musical experiences, it is the quality of the musical experience that in turn depends on the richness and vitality of the pedagogy, which will have maximum benefit for children. Hence the need to give the processes of teaching and learning the utmost attention.

Although I present the theories and philosophies that follow in this book in a (mostly) dispassionate way and try not to let my own viewpoints creep in, I will express my own values briefly here. Music enables us to present and revisit feelings that are deep and powerful. It enables us to express who we are and what our place is in the world. That is its value and the reason why music has such an important role in our lives. Why teach music then relates to the broader reasons behind education; why educate? The 'why educate' question asks us, in turn, to think carefully about what kind of society we want for the future. It is for everyone to arrive at their own image of the ideal society. In my view education should reach beyond just learning stuff and be about educating children to live well together with empathy and kindness, with care for one another, and for the planet. For this purpose children need an assured, valued sense of who they are in the world and to be able to think independently, imaginatively and to express themselves. Of course they need knowledge and skills to be able to make music for themselves and be more than listeners and consumers. But most importantly they need to know what to do with that knowledge and how to use those skills for the best purposes. No point in being able to recite rhythm names correctly if children are not given an opportunity to use them in meaningful musical experiences. I would also hope they learn to access all kinds of music, to be able to absorb its beauty, to participate and gain joy from participation.

Perspectives

Broadly speaking, there are three different perspectives which shape the process of teaching. I have already touched on these, but here I will expand on them. Simply stated, one perspective is concerned with 'putting in' and passing on musical traditions, another is concerned with 'drawing out' the musicality of the child and the third is concerned with teaching that is aware of social, political and cultural context. In practice of course most educators work within a combination of these perspectives.

The first, 'putting music in' and cultural traditions approach gives primary importance to the music that is to be learned. Here music is understood to be a set of skills, knowledge and cultural art forms – songs, pieces of music to listen to and perform – that education should pass on to children. The image of children is often described as a blank slate. The educator decides what is to be learnt and will convert the musical content into the forms that are thought to be most easily assimilated by the learning child. Musical literacy and introducing a selected repertoire of music to children may also be important. This approach is primarily intended to develop musicianship through singing and movement, and typically children are taken on a pathway that leads to the European classical tradition. The methods of music education introduced by Jaques-Dalcroze, Orff and Kodály aimed at handing on musical traditions.

The second, child-centred approach gives primary importance to the musicality, musical knowledge and abilities that the child already possesses. Music is conceived as a form of self-expression, a creative inner artistic force that teaching aims to release and shape. It will seek to draw out the spontaneous, creative and distinctive musical expressions of each child, as individuals. It is sometimes thought that in this approach the adult should not intervene, but that is rarely the case. The role of the teacher is to provide, stimulate, facilitate, observe and guide the child. The child-centred tradition in music education has its roots in the pioneers of education for younger children such as Froebel, Dewey, Montessori and Isaacs.

The third approach is concerned with the place of music within social and cultural contexts. From this viewpoint, the connections between music and sociocultural identity come to the fore. Kodály for example suggested that music education should instil in children a strong sense of their cultural heritage, mainly through its folk song traditions. More recently this perspective asks us to recognise that music education should attempt to dispel musical hierarchies for reasons of social justice and equality. The assumption of a common tradition of music based on European heritage as the basis of a music education is no longer appropriate given the increasing cultural diversity of school populations. It is fair to say that this third approach has made less impact on the field of early childhood music education. This perspective sees music education as much more than simply developing music skills or individual musical expressiveness, but as also concerned with wider social, cultural and political context of music and the children's and families' positions within musical cultures.

Each perspective differs in its philosophy of learning, its image of children, its conception of what music is and what is valued musically, and its conception of the role of the educator. As I stressed earlier, it is very unlikely that any teacher falls completely into one approach. However, the first music-centred approach dominates music education practice with young children. Typically it is the adult who makes the decisions about content and takes a strong lead in introducing and modelling that content. The children, or carers and children together, are expected to copy and join in. This is a model and rehearse approach evolved in school-based work with older children. The approach has been scaled down for early childhood in terms of the difficulty of its content but it still relies on a lead adult who performs the musical content for children who imitate.

Contrast this adult-centred approach with the approach to learning that is dominant in general early childhood practice. Here play is the medium for learning and the adult role shifts on its axis to one of encouraging play and listening, responding and supporting it. Although there has been research into children's musical play so that its processes are better understood, the pedagogies of music play are not widely incorporated into early childhood music education. We might wonder why early childhood music education, particularly with under-3-year-olds, has stronger roots in music education approaches that were evolved with older children and has been less influenced by general early childhood practice and its play-based pedagogies? Hopefully as you read this book answers to conundrums such as this will become clearer.

The different perspectives are often pitted in opposition to one another as child-centred in contrast to adult-centred, or progressive versus traditionalist. In my view, it is best to avoid these simple opposites and to think of a spectrum. There are situations when the most effective way to foster children's learning is for teachers to take the lead, to model and instruct and situations when the most suitable approach is to stand back and leave children to discover for themselves. It depends on what is being learnt, on the child's ability, personality, how they feel that day, what they already know, on the resources available, on the context and more. However, between the two ends of the spectrum there is every shade of interaction between adults and children. When there is reciprocal give and take between the contributions of adults and of children, this is when teaching and learning is likely to be most fruitful. These are the points of contact between education as discovery and education as transmission. However, these are the aspects of the learning-teaching process in music that tend to receive the least attention. Interestingly, as we will see, many of the philosophers and theorists of education, from their varying viewpoints and with differing explanations, focus on these points of contact between teacher and child and how educational interactions generate learning. Many of the music educators whose work I introduce in this book endeavour to capture the musical and pedagogical give-and-take between adults and children in the texts they have written.

Approach

Within these broad perspectives, there are varying approaches and methods. In many of the sections I refer to an 'approach' in educational practice. I use this term to describe a framework, both in theory and practice, which brings together values, knowledge and ideas. An approach guides and informs practice but with less definition than a method.

Method

Music education is characterised by a number of methods. I include the three most established methods, usually referred to by the names of their originators, Kodály, Orff and Dalcroze. Anyone who works in early childhood music will, I am certain, have come across one or all of these methods.

A method in education implies:

- a common approach in terms of content and teaching and learning strategies
- an underpinning philosophy and/or set of principles
- aims and goals that are worthwhile, and
- integrity (for example, they are non-commercial).

Music education methods typically share some common features in that they:

- introduce new learning content in a sequential way that is defined by the method
- use music that is considered to have a certain authenticity and value to young children, usually for example children's songs, folk music, often music of a particular heritage
- are based on theories of children's musicality and how they best learn
- encourage active participation in the form of moving, singing, playing instruments, in ways appropriate to the children's physical skills
- assume that children deserve to be educated to be active music-makers, not just music listeners.

For any method, there are convinced experts who promote a method's claimed values and provide training, passing on time-tested traditions of practice and activities to new teachers. Collective belief in the method can be strong. Its values and practices are to be accepted, largely without question. The risk is that the methods are viewed as pedagogies that should be adopted in their entirety, with reverence to the tradition. Here, however, I integrate them into the book as just one among many possibilities from which educators can learn and make independent decisions as to what they might select and adopt for their own practice. They should be viewed as a resource, not a dogmatic set of principles to be followed to the letter.

Personalised Method

Alongside these formalised, well-known methods experienced teachers are likely to have evolved their own, personalised methods. They will have accumulated components from many sources, quite likely taking from the established methods, from observations of the practice of other teachers, from reading and searching for materials and from trial and error. These highly personalised, blended methods become idiosyncratic and closely tied into the personality of the educator, the situations in which they teach and the children they work with. If something seems to work it is retained, what doesn't seem to work gets dropped. The flexibility, evaluation and constant evolution of the work is the strength of a personal method.

A possible risk is that the personalised method can become something of a rag bag, an add-on collection of activities that lacks a clear sense of overall purpose and direction. The risk, too, is that an individual method starts to crystallise and becomes fixed. The danger on another, more serious level is that 'what works' is assumed to be good teaching and this assumption closes down further questioning. The teacher starts to rationalise their approach drawing primarily on experience, cherry-picking theoretical ideas to bolster their experiential approach. Let me explore that further because I think it happens very commonly. Thinking back, I certainly fell into this model of practice. Reflective practice asks for an interplay and dialogue between theory and practice, not one leading the other.

So with either a grand method or a self-evolved method, important educational questions can get lost. Teaching the method can become the focus, rather than teaching children. Why is this? What 'works' is often limited to whether the children appear to be engaged, enjoying what we offer them and successfully achieving simple skills. A superficial level of behaviour on the part of the children becomes the assessment of whether the activity has 'worked'. The educator may not be asking themselves deeper questions as to whether the children (and perhaps their accompanying carers as well in the case of babies) have genuinely expanded their ability and understanding in any new directions. Have they, for example, expanded their ability to sing, move rhythmically, understand musical concepts, create their own music, use their musical imaginations or experienced music that is not familiar to them? Have they all had a meaningful, artistic musical experience? It also avoids the deeper questions of what is it that these children in front of me here and now need musically? How do I connect with their musicality, with their musical lives and how might I, as a teacher, take the children in musical directions that are valuable for them and for the communities and societies they live in? Teaching based on continual search for how to do it better is not always comfortable; it asks for honest appraisal and the ability to make changes. Change involves taking risks. Things can go badly; and if parents are paying, or the nursery manager or headteacher is looking on, taking risks might have wider consequences. It is understandable that it can be safer to stay with the tried and tested activities.

What is Included in This Book

This book is intended to be an introduction to a range of theories and philosophies that have influenced the course of early childhood music education. There are signposts to further reading those who wish to go on and research a topic in more depth and detail. Methods and pedagogical approaches should be viewed as frameworks, as sources that can inspire and inform. By bringing these together in one book I can highlight the connections, contrasts and relationships between different theories. Common ideas start to emerge. I explain some of the criticisms and suggest what the shortcomings might be. I can also put these ideas and approaches into their historical context and show the historical progression of ideas.

I have had to make some selections, however. Those selections reflect my position in the UK and also what I considered to be most relevant and useful. Some readers outside the UK will consider, I am certain, that I have left out important approaches or that I include some that they would consider marginal. Also, this book is aimed at general music educators, and less for educators interested in the early stages of learning an instrument. For that reason, for example, I do not include the Suzuki method because it is focussed on learning an instrument.

I have not included any contributions from recent brain research. This is not because I do not find this research interesting and potentially valuable, but because I think it is as yet too specialised to offer any broader understandings of learning and teaching in music. Brain research tends to be called up for its persuasive power rather than because, at present, it can genuinely inform practice. Besides, there is no pedagogical approach or method informed by neuroscience theory and this is a book about existing practices, not hypothetical practice.

For a similar reason, there is almost nothing about music technology in this book, even though the advance of technologies means that music is even more present in children's lives and even more accessible via touchscreen technologies and small, hand-held devices. If I had been writing about educational approaches I would like to see evolving, then music technology would certainly be included. But to date, there is little or no work in early childhood music education that makes use of music technology in a considered pedagogical way. Teachers might play backing tracks to accompany their singing, or search for YouTube clips to play to children, but this is not yet a defined teaching approach. Nor is there anything about music education that addresses the pressing issue of climate change and sustainability, except for one short section on eco-literate music education.

Age Range

This book covers the age range from birth to around 8 years. In countries where formal schooling does not begin until the ages of 6 or 7 years, the early childhood phase usually extends from birth to those ages. In the UK, which, to be blunt, shoves children into formal schooling at around 5 years or even younger, early childhood usually refers to the age phase from birth to 5 years. So, given the starting age of formal schooling in the UK, this book will be informative for British teachers working in the first years of schooling.

However the age range covered by the term 'early childhood' in education has shifted at various times. During the twentieth century, even as late as the 1990s, early childhood usually covered the age range 3 to 8 years, with barely any attention given to under-3-year-olds. More recently, since the 2000s, the age phase has shifted downwards in age, with much interest in the earliest years of birth to 3 years so that early childhood usually designates the birth to 5 years age phase. However that shift has resulted in less focus on the ages 5 to 8 years. Unfortunately, this rapid expansion of music practice for babies and toddlers, with accompanying adults, has not been matched by careful research into pedagogical approaches. Practice with under-3s is playing catch-up in terms of evolving understandings of how best to work in this phase, particularly in work which is dyadic – that is, includes the carers with the under-3-year-olds.

Scenarios

Each section that follows includes a short description of practice. These scenarios are included to illustrate what the theory, philosophy or method looks like in practice. As often as possible, these are taken directly from the music education books by the historical authors I mentioned earlier, either paraphrased or quoted directly. In a few cases where there was not an obvious text to draw on, I have created the description myself. I have tried to ensure the scenarios include children of different ages in different situations, in order to be representative.

The scenarios also try to be representative of different contexts. Early childhood music takes place in a wide variety of different contexts. It may be integrated into daycare or nursery provision, woven into the ongoing play-based practice or it may take place in a dedicated music session, with a lead adult and group of children. It may also be offered as private music classes; typically attended by parent with child, often framed by a particular named, commercialised approach.

Image of Childhood

Underlying all educational questions is a conception of children and childhood. In each section I have described the image of childhood that underpins the theory or philosophy. Childhood itself is now understood as a sociocultural construct, meaning that the experience of being a child is not fixed and universal but variable across time and place. Reflecting on the conception of childhood can be a valuable means to highlight certain assumptions that underlie and influence practice.

These images might be of the child as a blank slate, an evolutionary primitive, an unfolding moral and spiritual being, as a little scientist exploring nature or as rich with inborn potential and individual competences. Present-day constructions of musical childhoods may still echo with historical images. Later theorists adopted ideas of cognitive abilities as emerging with biological development or of the mind working something like a machine. Newer representations construct children as more active, knowledgeable and socially competent than older discourses allowed. Models of development that suggested children were all the same and developed in the same way came to be prominent in the understanding of children and continue to have a strong influence on images of children. But the stronghold of developmentalism came in for criticism. Models of development were replaced with more fluid, flexible understandings of how children mature and how each child lives in different circumstances that influence their development. Nowadays there is increased anxiety around children, that they are vulnerable, at risk and need a high level of protection and investment. A common image of childhood that underlies practice today is that little children are precious, and should live in a protected, happy and fun-filled environment. It is also important to note that contemporary childhood studies are drawing attention to cultural variations in images of childhood and these are just beginning to impinge on music education practice.

Linked with this image of childhood is the fact that many of the older texts automatically refer to the child as 'he'. We would now avoid using only the male pronoun in this way. However I have left the quotes in their original versions.

A Chronology

What follows is a simple chronology that sketches the main changes through the decades from the 1900 onwards. Sketch is the key word here, for this is only intended as a rough guide. Nevertheless, a chronology has its uses. It highlights some of the major themes and how those themes have changed over time. The first half of the twentieth century saw the work of philosopher-pedagogues. In music education the major philosopher-pedagogues were Jaques-Dalcroze, Orff and Kodály. From early childhood education I have picked out those philosopher-pedagogues who both advanced new versions of early childhood education and whose work led to a particular contribution to early childhood music: Froebel, Dewey, Montessori and Isaacs.

Alongside these early approaches, until about the late 1950s the dominant theory of learning from psychologists was behaviourism; a simple conception of learning as a response to a stimulus. A major shift took place in the 1960s and 1970s, prompted by psychologists' new interests in cognitive process and development. These new ways of thinking about learning started to inform music educators' work and some of the most interesting and informative work by music educators working with young children, in my opinion, emanates from this period. Many of the advances during the latter part of the twentieth century then revolved round the central theme of constructivism with its basic thesis that children construct their understanding of the world they experience. These ideas folded back into the major methods of music education which adapted and evolved accordingly.

One of the problems I encountered, however, in setting out a timeline is that there is a lag between theories arising from the work of psychologists and their application to education, particularly to music education, which is often, to be honest, some way behind the curve. There is also a lag between methods being evolved in their countries of origin, and their wider dissemination to other countries. My dilemma was whether to give the chronology as the time when the psychologist was writing about their theory or the pioneer devising their new method in the country of origin – or when the new ideas started to be applied by music educators or spread to other countries? I've mostly focused on when theories were integrated into music education or methods spread to other countries.

1900–1950

Behaviourist theories dominated the conception of learning throughout the first half of the twentieth century.

At the turn of the twentieth century a new way of thinking about children and schooling began to emerge, loosely called progressive education and also known as the New Education movement. The ideas and practice of New Education aimed both to reform traditional education methods and to explore experimental pedagogies.

- 1900s: Jaques-Dalcroze developed eurhythmics which soon spread internationally.
- 1920s: Orff developed his creative music and dance approach which was later adapted for children as Orff Schulwerk.
- 1940s: Kodály introduced his singing-based method into Hungarian schools.

1950–2000

Progressive, child-centred approaches that were informed increasingly by Piaget's theories of cognition started to influence mainstream infant and nursery practice.

- 1960s: Developmental cognitive learning theories inspired music education research. Teachers were encouraged to think of childhood in developmental psychology terms and to adjust their teaching. There was growing interest in children's musical development and their musical thinking.
- 1960s–1970s: Kodály and Orff methods spread internationally and began to incorporate ideas from developmental psychology.

- 1970s: Theories of children's learning leant increasingly towards constructivism. Children construct their own understanding, building on what they already know. Music education practice started to be informed by constructivist theories of learning and teaching, notably from Bruner. The creative music movement arose in infant schools (5 to 7 years). There were tensions between the new creative music movement, and traditional, subject-centred approaches. A new field of research with babies started to reveal their competences.
- 1980s: Theories of social constructivism expand the idea of constructivism by emphasising the role of context and social interaction. There was a growing interest in World music and how to incorporate multicultural music in education.

2000–Present

- 2000s: Grand theories of musical development were replaced by an emphasis on social and cultural aspects of music learning. The result was a multiplicity of theoretical thinking about how young children's experiences from social and cultural perspectives could be understood in relation to learning. Continuing research into adult infant interaction revealed the competences of babyhood, including musical competences. Practice expanded downwards in age to under-3s and there was a rapid increase in mother and baby music sessions.
- 2010s: There was growing pressure for musical learning to be identified in relation the extrinsic benefits of music.
- 2020s: Music education must adapt to a series of crises and address social and global issues.

Reference

Biesta, G. J. J. (2013). *The Beautiful Risk of Education*. Boulder, CO: Paradigm Publishers.

Part I

The first two parts of this book look broadly at two historical theories of learning. Although both these theories seem outdated when described in their original form, their legacies still resonate in current music education practice.

Evolutionary theories proposed that the starting points of music learning for very young children match the starting points of the cultural history of Western music. Both have 'primitive' beginnings, to use the language of evolutionary theory. Therefore, it was thought that young children should start their music education at the beginning of music's history, with its original elements and forms.

Behaviourist psychology proposed that learning music consists of becoming proficient in a range of musical behaviours; those behaviours would consist of observable musical skills and straightforward, factual knowledge. Behaviourist theory says that children learn best by imitating what an adult tells or models for them. This pedagogical approach continues to be a mainstay of music education practice.

1 Musical Learning as Recapitulation

> Then in a vision ... I saw my little pupils going back to their first music not to the Greeks, but much, much further back, even to primitive man and the early savages .... Being little savages they can understand savage music. I shall find the child's own savage level, and lift him gradually up to higher forms; and he shall understand each stage as he reaches it, for his power will grow with it, and his work will always be at his own level. The natural evolution of music shall be my guide in leading the child from the simple to the complex.
> (Coleman, 1922, p. 29)

Although we may cringe, laugh or be outraged at how Satis Coleman refers to children as little savages and to man as primitive, this quote illustrates the idea of recapitulation that shaped early theories of how children developed musically and informed music education practice. In the late nineteenth century Charles Darwin began looking at children's development with his theory of evolution in mind. Darwin believed that by studying the development of children he could describe the evolutionary history of the human species. This belief expanded into the idea that as they learn, children 'recap' the history of human culture and that therefore educational practice should follow the same path. Satis Coleman's book has the subtitle: *a plan of training based on the natural evolution of music*.

Written in 1922, Satis Coleman's words are easily dismissed as outdated. But the idea of recapitulation filtered into the music education methods from the early part of the twentieth century – as we will see in Part II – and its vestiges remain today in approaches to curriculum design and pedagogy.

Recapitulation Theory

Granville Stanley Hall (1844–1924) was one of the leading American psychologists of the late nineteenth and early twentieth century. He believed that growing children retrace the evolutionary path of the human species as a whole and that there is one-to-one correspondence between childhood stages and the evolution of the human race. The core idea is that children repeat in their development the physiological and cultural development of the species.

So, whether learning to walk, progressing in play, or becoming musically competent, children progress through stages that mirror the history not only of their biological species (from motions of swimming fish, through crawling, to upright posture) but also of their cultural race, from savage to civilised. Children were described as primitive, thought to be akin to ancient man and people who were considered to be not culturally advanced. Nowadays we find the thought of attributing the characteristic 'primitive' to any people, of whatever age and cultural-social background, to be deeply unpleasant and prejudicial.

The idea of recapitulation was adopted to explain cultural progression, including music. Western art music was assumed to represent the pinnacle of musical achievement and other musical cultures of the world – including folk musics – represented stages of earlier cultural evolution that could be aligned with earlier stages of European music history. That Western art music, particularly music in the classical tradition, is assumed to sit atop a musical hierarchy, remains in music education thinking, even though that assumption is now heavily criticised.

Stanley Hall believed that recapitulation theory provided a rational, natural explanation for children's psychological development. While his core theory was subsequently disputed, he was one of the first to believe that psychology could inform education and that education should be adapted to reflect children's psychological development. For Hall, schooling needed to match the child's recapitulation journey and allow the child to engage in activities that completed proper development at each stage. Hence, even savagery – an early stage of humankind, so it was thought at that time – ought to be accommodated through opportunities enabled by the natural world; playing outdoors and hunting, for example. If not, suppressed 'natural' expressions and arrested development would, it was thought, cause problems later in adulthood. So, broadly speaking, his ideas encouraged an early childhood education that was responsive to children's naturalness and allowed for play, spontaneity and freedom, even if the detail of his theory was less helpful.

Recommendations for Music Education

Although primarily a psychologist, Stanley Hall also had some definite recommendations for music education. He thought any kind of formal and intellectual approach to learning music for young children was wrong.

> The rule of nature is sing, sing, sing. It is just as preposterous to teach notes before teaching the power to sing, as it would be to teach reading before the child can talk ... The function of music is to balance the soul and give it rhythm. Rhythm, which is the mother of prose, poetry, and music, gives the note thought and sets the pace for all our psychic operations.
>
> (Stanley Hall, 1908, p. 360)

Musical Learning as Recapitulation   19

Evolutionary theory permeated various music teaching pedagogies between 1890 to the 1930s. A generation of music educators believed that children pass through stages of musical development equivalent to that of primitive societies as they progressed towards more 'culturally sophisticated' music. Therefore children should be provided with musical experiences that match the cultural period of their developmental stage. Leading music educators tried to organise curricula for children as a progression through the epochs of past musical cultures.

Ideas of cultural evolutionism combined with recapitulation theory from psychology also suggested that the spontaneous musical expressions of children at play could be compared with the musics of so-called primitive peoples. This comparison, they thought, could confirm how the European child passed through stages of musical ability that matched earlier stages of European cultural history or to the living music of non-European peoples and uneducated European peasants.

The Theory in Practice

One striking example of evolutionary theory applied to music education practice is Satis Coleman's (1878–1961) 'creative music' approach. A quote from her book stands at the start of this section. Coleman evolved her approach for children aged 3 years and upwards. The children, as she explained, should live the evolution of music through making their own instruments (the drum stage), rhythmic movement in dancing (rhythmic stage) leading to singing and performance. She believed that in the natural evolution of music, rhythm came first, then melody, then harmony and then tone colour and shading.

A distinctive aspect of her approach was the construction of instruments by the children from found materials with which the children then improvised and incorporated into song and dance performances.

> The Drum Stage – since all children ... love to beat something and make a noise, this tendency presented itself as one means of developing the rhythmic sense. After having the child use his hands and feet in the making of rhythmic sounds, my next step was to stimulate his curiosity about the kinds of sounds that were produced when different surfaces were struck, leading from flat surfaces to the resonant sound of concave and hollow bodies. I had procured ... an imitation hollow stump and a hollow log, and the children were interested in the sound produced by striking these ... The suggestion they might be able to make drums was received with delight ... The discussion of what we would use to make them and how, aroused their curiosity and led to the investigation of what primitive and other people had used to make drums and what available material there was for us ... One child made a drum from a chopping bowl, another from a coconut shell; a spice box provide the

right size for a tabor ... they used them in beating song and dance rhythms, in echoing the rhythms of melodies played by others, and in improvising rhythms. They were interested in the drum codes of savages and made drum codes of their own.

(Coleman, 1922, p. 34)

The children progressed from percussive instruments through explorations of making blown instruments and then stringed.

Key Text

Satis Coleman. (1922). *Creative Music for Children: A plan of training based on the natural evolution of music including the making and playing of instruments, dancing, singing, poetry*. New York: G. P. Putnam's Sons.

Image of Childhood

Stanley Hall regarded children as developing through stages. The first stage, 3 years until 6 or 7 years, corresponded to the primitive man stage in evolution. In this stage children experience life through the physical senses, similar to animals, their physical growth is rapid and energy levels are high. Young children have not yet developed the ability to reason and lack social skills. Stanley Hall argued that formal education should only begin at the age of 8 years since children only acquire reasoning skills at this age.

Comments and Connections

Evolutionary approaches to musical development centred on rhythm because in rhythm, it was thought, lie the origins of music. Young children should begin with rhythmic movement and also with chants and drones and simple musical forms that are representative of folk music, medieval music and the music of non-European people. Although theories of children's development as recapitulation may have been long superseded, vestiges of this theory can be found in present-day music education practices. Jaques-Dalcroze, for example, emphasised rhythmic movement and dance in his eurhythmics training; a method that has had a profound influence on later methods.

Satis Coleman's work anticipated Orff in her focus on improvisation with instruments. Carl Orff's pedagogical method (see p. 74) integrated Stanley Hall's ideas on recapitulation theory via the ethnomusicology (or comparative musicology as it was referred to at the time) of Curt Sachs, who was known to Orff. Orff evolved an approach based on progression from oral/bodily musical expression to improvisation on percussion instruments. According to Orff's ideas the child should progress from simple vocalisations, moving on to pentatonic and modal forms related to European folk music. Only then could the 'intellectual' harmonies and structures of Western art music be gradually introduced. This progression from instinctive to intellectual fits recapitulation theory. In Kodály's approach there are similar ideas of starting with simple two-tone melodies, rooted in folk music and a gradual progression through simply phrased and structured songs.

Embedded in ideas of recapitulation theory is a historical view of music that holds inbuilt racial hierarchies that we now know to be deeply unjust, and yet these linger, woven into practices and ideas about music education. At root these historical approaches to music education were based on the assumed superiority of white European music. While we may obviously avoid words like primitive or savages which Coleman used, she was simply using terms that represented the understanding of hierarchy and 'other' musics common in the 1920s together with images of childhood. Today they stand out as obviously prejudicial. In a section towards the end of the book I consider in detail the progression of theory and practice from these past ideas of recapitulation theory through multiculturalism and on to contemporary theories of decolonisation.

Bibliography

Coleman, S. (1922). *Creative Music for Children: A plan of training based on the natural evolution of music including the making and playing of instruments, dancing, singing, poetry*. New York: G. P. Putnam's Sons.

Shevock, D. (2015). Satis Coleman – a spiritual philosophy for music education. *Music Educators Journal*, 102(1), 56–61.

Stanley Hall, G. (1908). The psychology of music and the light it throws upon music education. *The Pedagogical Seminary*, 15(3), 358–364.

2 Behaviourism: Learning through Imitation and Reinforcement

> The simplest and most satisfactory view is that thought is simply behavior – verbal or nonverbal, covert or overt. It is not some mysterious process responsible for behavior but the very behavior itself in all the complexity of its controlling relations.
>
> (B. F. Skinner, 1957, p. 449)

Behaviourism is a broad, general theory to which several theorists and researchers have contributed, rather than a theory arising from the work of one person. A number of influential learning theories were developed under the banner of behaviourism between 1900 and 1950.

According to behaviourists what goes on in the mind is impossible to study so they focus on the behaviours that can be observed. For behaviourists, a change in behaviour is the sign that learning has taken place.

Theory

Behaviourism is an approach to learning that has its origin in research with animals and studies of their behaviour. Behaviourists argued that the laws of learning were the same for all species and so by studying learning in non-human animals, the early behaviourists thought they were identifying the basic processes that were key to human learning. Pavlov's famous experiments with dogs during the 1890s, conditioning them to anticipate food when a bell was rung, demonstrated an association between the bell and food. This is a very simple learning mechanism based on stimulus and response. Learning is viewed, in essence, as a function of change with what are, in very simple terms, stimuli (for example, the teacher claps a rhythm) and responses (the children imitate the rhythm clapping).

Burrhus Frederic Skinner (1904–1990) advanced behaviourist thinking in the 1940s through his studies of laboratory rats in specially designed cages. In one experiment the rats could discover by accident that a lever would release food, but then, over time, they learnt how to press the lever. The new learning was motivated by the reward of food; the reinforcement. This process was termed 'operant conditioning' (Aubrey and

DOI: 10.4324/9781003331193-4

Riley, 2022). He went on to experiment with the details of the conditioning process. For example he discovered that the reinforcement needed to occur promptly after the learned behaviour (pressing the lever) and that it needed to be consistent. Intermittent rewards did not reinforce the learning so effectively.

Transferred to education, the theory suggests that the teacher must observe the children's behaviour and reinforce the desired and 'correct' behaviour, with praise or some other kind of reward (or deter any undesired behaviour by withholding praise or commenting to correct the behaviour). Thus behaviour is shaped by feedback and positive reinforcement. The simple underlying idea is that children act to gain reward; the equivalent of a food reward when a rat learns to press the lever.

There is another key element in behavioural learning theory. For Skinner learning should be broken down into small steps and ordered sequentially and incrementally so that success is as guaranteed as possible (Skinner, 1957). Then each step can be rewarded and learning is positively reinforced. Following this pedagogical principle, the teacher should select learning content and sequence it, following a predetermined and consistent pathway. Moreover, they actively direct the child by maintaining control over the content, the pace and the sequence of learning. It is thus teacher-directed learning rather than learner-centred.

The Theory in Practice

> *A teacher is working with a class of 5-year-olds. He claps a short rhythm pattern and asks the children to copy and repeat it. He repeats the echo clapping activity several times and introduces rhythm patterns that gradually increase in difficulty. There are many repetitions of those patterns so that the children can practise clapping the rhythm patterns with increasing accuracy. The teacher praises the children when they clap the rhythm patterns correctly.*

The educator:

- models the musical skill
- repeats to reinforce and provide practice
- increases the difficulty of skill and complexity of rhythm with small, progressive steps, and
- provides continuous positive reinforcement, with words of praise or awards.

The children imitate and repeat the actions of the teacher, and receive immediate feedback on their performance of the rhythm patterns. Learning is defined as a change in behaviour, a change in what the children do or say. The teacher might follow the activity with a question (stimulus) and answer (response) session to prompt learning. Typically the questions are closed questions with one correct answer. If the children fail to give the correct answer, the teacher will repeat the question and then prompt and cue the children until they find the answer.

Establishing Routines

Because behaviourism reinforces learning through repeated actions these techniques are often applied in the management of children's behaviour. Typically a session with a larger group or whole class may begin with the kind of copy, quick response and repeat activity described above in order to gather and focus the children's attention. Equally, verbal rewards, star charts or stickers are all simple incentives systems based on reward – or punishment by withdrawal of privileges – that encourage children to conform to the expectations and routines of a session.

Cues are sometimes used by the teacher to serve a dual function as a learning activity that also establishes working routines. For example, the teacher may establish a routine that if she claps a rhythm pattern at any point in the lesson the children are expected to stop their ongoing activity, respond by imitating the clapping pattern and pay attention.

Rewards and Motivation

Although Skinner and other behavioural psychologists experimented with animals, some of their findings regarding rewards and their effect on motivation and behaviour are relevant to the education of children. They experimented with different timings and patterns of reward. For example, they found that reinforcement is more effective if it is received immediately after the desired behaviour, rather than being delayed.

Another useful aspect of behavioural theory concerned the frequency of reinforcement. For example, if a child is praised every time they do something, the praise soon loses value. But at the same time, if rarely praised, the child feels under-valued. In both cases the behaviour weakens and disappears. Interestingly, and perhaps contrary to what we might think, rewards given variably have the greatest effect. Reinforcement at the start of a new learning process might have a positive effect, but thereafter variable reward seems to have a longer-lasting effect. Educators are often very enthusiastic in their praise but might think again about when and how often they are providing praise.

Rewards must be managed carefully if they are to increase children's intrinsic motivation and reduce their extrinsic motivation. Intrinsic motivation is children's own sense of pleasure, and satisfaction at being able to achieve something. Extrinsic motivators such as praise and stickers can be useful short-term rewards but should be withdrawn to increase children's own sense of competence and ability.

Key Text

Burrhus Frederic Skinner. (1974). *About Behaviorism*. New York: Knopf Doubleday Publishing.

Image of Childhood

According to a behaviourist view, the child comes into the world as an empty vessel, often referred to as a *tabula rasa* (blank slate). Knowledge and skills are external to the child and need to be handed on to them through a simple process of transmission. The child is viewed as passive and their learning will be shaped through positive reinforcement. Learning, from the behaviourist perspective, is what happens to children as a result of their external experiences.

Comments and Connections

When behaviourist approaches to learning are described, particularly when their origins in animal experiments are explained, they can sound mechanical and outdated. Yet, in reality, many pedagogical strategies that have come to be familiar in music education practice are strongly behaviourist. The children are often taught as one of a group or a whole class. The expectation is that the teacher will take a strong lead, modelling musical activities and the children imitate in unison with singing or performing rhythmic actions.

It is true that learning musical skills can be effectively achieved through model, imitation, repeat and practice strategies. Behaviourist learning approaches also guide the development of sequenced and structured curricula that aim to build learning step-by-step. In particular if children find a certain skill more challenging, or they are children with certain learning needs, then a didactic, step-by-step approach that relies on drill and practice may help them to acquire skills and make progress.

The main feature of a curriculum based on behaviourist principles is that it defines learning in terms of what the children can do, the actions and what can be observed – rather, than, in terms of what children understand. Tasks that require more complex thinking and higher mental processes are not, generally, well learned through behaviourist methods. They require more attention to how children perceive, process and make sense of what they are experiencing. The 5-year-olds described in the echo clapping scenario earlier can perform the rhythm patterns correctly by rote, but little more. If they are to understand how rhythm is related to pulse, or to rhythm syllable sounds or visual symbols – how to create rhythm patterns of their own or play them independently – then much more attention needs to be given to pedagogical strategies that will promote children's musical understanding.

So behaviourist theory is criticised because it is too simple to explain all the ins and outs of musical learning. In contrast to other theories, it is focused on the external, observable behaviours with little attention given to the inner processes of learning and understanding. It does not help children to identify and draw together connections and associations between different elements of what they are being taught (something that leads to genuine musical understanding). It allows few opportunities for exploration and discovery through play, or self-initiated activity. Particularly if they are being taught as one of a group or a whole class the children may have little opportunity to make choices or decisions independently. They are not invited to contribute their own ideas, to explore or to create. They are, thus, unlikely to develop qualities such as critical thinking and self-expression. To understand children's thinking and how it changes we need theories that are more concerned with cognitive process such as the ones described later in this book. Critics would also say a behaviourist approach does not cater for the differences between children, it treats them as if they are all the same. It provides little attention to individual needs and interests.

The learning approach therefore is closely related to how music is viewed as a subject for learning. If music education is seen primarily as about learning to perform music, to sing songs accurately, to perform rhythms and learning the basics of notation, acquiring a fixed set of skills and knowledge in other words, then behavioural approaches will be adopted and are likely to be successful. In later sections we will encounter alternative ways of viewing music as a subject for learning.

Bibliography

Aubrey, K. and Riley, A. (2022). B. F. Skinner, The Father of Operant Conditioning. In K. Aubrey and A. Riley, *Understanding and Using Educational Theories*, 3rd edition, pp. 69–83. London: Sage.

Skinner, B. F. (1957). *Verbal Behavior*. New York: Appleton-Century-Crofts.

Part II

Part II discusses four historical educational thinkers: Froebel, from the nineteenth century (1782–1852), and Montessori, Dewey and Isaacs, who worked in the first half of the twentieth century. Froebel, Montessori and Isaacs were early childhood educators who developed innovative pedagogies for young children. Dewey was less directly involved with early childhood education, however he set up an experimental school at the university of Chicago based on his philosophy for education.

Each of these educational thinkers highlighted what they saw as the shortcomings of education and proposed alternative approaches. At the times and in the places they were working, the educational emphasis was on rote teaching, drill and memorisation. Each, in their own way, proposed radical changes that allowed children freedom for play, exploration, discovery and social interaction. After the First World War, in the 1920s, there was a strong sense that the world was changing and education needed to change with it. The ideas and practices of the New Education movement included both an attitude of reforming for the better and an interest in experimental curricula and pedagogies. The innovative ideas for education from that time continue to have relevance today.

None of these major figures from the history of early childhood education developed a specific pedagogy for music education, although they all offered thinking on music education, some in more detail than others. Froebel produced a book of mother and baby songs, Montessori invited two colleagues to work on a music approach to incorporate into her nursery pedagogy, Isaacs was a pianist who played for children's movement influenced by Dalcroze eurhythmics and Dewey worked closely with a music educator, Eleanor Smith, in his experimental school. However, as well as these direct contributions to music education, their philosophies and theories of education have been broadly influential on music education pedagogies and practices. In each section I include the work of a music educator who has interpreted their ideas into practice, sometimes contemporary with the main theorist, sometimes more recent. The legacy of these educators inspires and challenges us to continue examining assumptions underlying current trends in early childhood music education.

DOI: 10.4324/9781003331193-5

3 Friedrich Froebel: Learning through Play

> Play is the highest level of child development. It is the spontaneous expression of thought and feeling. ... It constitutes the source of all that can benefit the child ... At this age play is never trivial; it is serious and deeply significant.
> (Froebel in Lilley, 1967, p. 84)

Friedrich Froebel was one of the first to emphasise the value of play and its contribution to children's social and emotional development and learning. In the early 1800s, when Froebel established what he called *kindergarten*, young children were taught by rote and expected to be passive, so his philosophy for education and new methods represented a radical change. The name kindergarten signifies both a garden *for* children, where they can play in a natural environment, as well as a garden *of* children, in which they are cared for and grow. His kindergarten had three main components: creative play; singing and dancing; and observing and nurturing the natural environment.

In the mid-1800s the Froebel Society was established in England and offered training in the Froebelian approach. In 1894 the Froebel Institute opened in London and continues today, actively supporting research and practice based on Froebelian principles and bringing them in line with contemporary early childhood education. Froebel's play-based principles of learning have been hugely influential on early childhood education practice.

Froebel wrote a book of mother and infant songs and had strong views about the value of songs and singing in the education of young children. He has made a lasting contribution to early childhood music education practice.

Friedrich Froebel (1782–1852)

Friedrich Froebel was born in Thuringia, now part of Germany. He had a number of different occupations before taking up a position as a teacher in a school that followed the progressive principles of the Swiss educator, Johann Pestalozzi. Froebel then set up his own school in 1816. Later in 1831 he was invited by the Swiss government to become involved in training teachers to work with young children and in 1837 established a school for young children that he later named a kindergarten.

DOI: 10.4324/9781003331193-6

Philosophy

Froebel's philosophy was based on a creative, child-centred approach that placed play and spiritual growth at the centre. He believed, based on his religious beliefs, that everything in the universe is connected and that the more one is aware of this unity, the deeper the understanding of oneself, of others, of nature and the wider world. Underpinning his belief in unity was a conception of the whole child; that all aspects of a child's life, thoughts, feelings, actions and relationships, are interrelated.

Froebel respected children as independent, learning through their own actions. He emphasised learning as the gradual unfolding of understanding from within the child, rather than learning being imposed from without. He saw that play made important contributions to young children's development and learning across all domains; physical, social, emotional and intellectual. He also saw that self-initiated play activities develop qualities such as determination, concentration and persistence. He placed value on the social aspects of play, and how children develop relationships based on empathy, a sense of fairness and care for others.

Creativity for Froebel was core to being human and a fundamental dimension to learning. It enables children to connect their inner worlds of thought and feeling to their outer world of experiences, to think about those connections and to endeavour to make sense of them. While he valued children's unique individual creativity he also valued the creative arts and he thought that art, music, song and dance should all be part of the kindergarten world.

Children should have freedom to play, but he believed that they should also become aware of the limitations and constraints on freedom. This tension between freedom and constraint was an important aspect of creativity for Froebel. Adults play an important role in guiding children's play so that they might achieve their intentions, but at the same time, assist them to become aware of the limitations on their freedom.

Principles

According to Froebel's philosophy, children should have rich, first-hand, sensory experiences which start with their own interests and then move on to new possibilities. Children should have free access to open-ended resources (simple, good quality), allowing children choice, control and ownership of their play. Play needs time.

Self-activity

Froebel stressed the importance of innate motivation that he termed 'self-activity' and stated that children should have the freedom to follow their own motivations.

Creativity and Symbols

Froebel noticed that children often took objects and used them in pretend play as completely different objects. So, for instance, if educational percussion instruments are made available to children for free play, they may use them in pretend play and the drums become bowls and beaters become spoons. He also suggested that the objects themselves may contain universal concepts and therefore thought that certain items could be given to children to play with that would enable them to experience these truths. For example, spheres for Froebel represented the unity that was so central to his spiritual outlook and a cube represented diversity with its many sides and corners.

Froebel realised that when children are sung to and told stories, these experiences feed characters and narratives into their own creative play and make-believe. Creative activities are valued because they allow children to make connections between their inner feelings and ideas and their outer, real-world experiences.

The Surmise

In attempting to explain something Froebel noticed that children will arrive at a tentative explanation that he termed 'a surmise'. This term describes the tension between what they know and do not know yet, but are struggling to work out for themselves. The idea of surmise is linked with creativity, imagination and problem solving.

Nature

Children should experience and be at one with nature. The outdoor world is a place for activity, curiosity and play. This principle connects strongly with Froebel's beliefs in spirituality, beauty and harmony.

The Gifts and Occupations

Somewhat in contrast to free outdoor exploration, Froebel designed a range of educational materials or *gifts* as he termed them. The gifts included differently shaped objects, blocks and spheres, that were quite small and precise. They were designed to be played with, but through that play to stimulate thinking and learning, particularly of form, structure and number concepts. He also designed 'occupations' such as weaving, cutting and sewing to encourage dexterity and creativity.

Songs and Musical Play

Froebel considered that there was an important connection between songs and rhymes and the actions and movements that accompany them. He wrote songs for young children based on their everyday interests and incorporated actions, mainly finger play, that imitated objects and activities from everyday rural life.

Role of the Adult

The role of the educator is to be a sensitive partner in play who offers freedom with well-judged guidance. The educator should convey values of love, sympathy, humility, cooperation with others and obedience. Froebel stressed that women should be trained as early childhood educators – a gender emphasis we might challenge today, but the importance he placed on training remains highly relevant.

Key Text

Friedrich Froebel. (1855). *The Education of Man* (trans. J. Jarvis). New York: A. Lovell and Company. (Original work first published in 1827.)

Image of Childhood

> Children are like tiny flowers: They are varied and need care, but each is beautiful alone and glorious when seen in the community of peers.
> (Froebel in Lilley, 1967)

Froebel's introduction of the kindergarten movement positioned children as tiny flowers, in a state of natural and divine goodness, free and innocent. Childhood was seen as separate from adulthood and the kindergarten was an idealised, protected space where adults nurture children. Natural growth arose from the freedom of children as they were encouraged to follow their own interests.

The Philosophy in Practice

The cultivation of creativity was central to Froebelian philosophy, and music – in particular songs and rhymes with finger play – was an important component of his educational approach. Froebel believed that music contributed to the general education of children and had a beneficial effect on children's character, rather than being merely a starting point for those who would play an instrument or study music seriously.

Working with a visual artist and a musician Froebel wrote poems which were then illustrated and set to music to create the book *Mutter und Koselieder* published in 1844. In 1906 the book was translated into English under the title *Mother-Play and Nursery Songs* with a sub-heading *Noble Culture of Child Life*. One of the purposes of the book was to develop a child's 'body, limbs and senses' through fingerplays, simple rhythmic movements to the songs and games played with their mother. Each rhyme is accompanied by an illustration and a commentary. The commentaries discuss the training of the senses and also the development of social empathy and awareness through the singing of songs. Although this book was originally intended for use at home, in family situations, the singing of songs, particularly simple action songs and rhymes, became a regular activity in Froebel nurseries and has become a mainstay of general early childhood practice.

Froebel proposed that the act of singing to babies was a means to convey motherly feelings of love and care. He also believed that the content of his songs helped both women and babies to understand their place, role and purpose in the world and their connectedness to the natural environment and to the divine creator. Froebel proposed that anyone working with young children needed to be specially trained to be confident at singing and knowing a repertoire of children's songs. Froebel's mother had died when he was a baby which may go some way to explaining why he promoted women as teachers at a time when teaching was largely seen as a male occupation and also why he was motivated to emphasise the value of mother-infant songs.

The Babysong Project

In 2013 researchers at the Froebel Institute and Canterbury Christ Church University, England established the Babysong Project. The project team worked with daycare practitioners to explore ways in which singing and song could be incorporated into their everyday care and activity with babies. It aimed to challenge a growing tendency towards a functional approach to daycare practice with babies and very young children. The project hoped to foster a closer, more intimate approach to interactions between practitioners and babies in their care.

The Spectrum of Song

Central to the project was the idea of a spectrum of song that ranged from infant-direct speech and playful vocalisations to 'singese' (infant-directed vocalisations using a singing voice) and the singing of known songs. They explored ways that the practitioners could integrate the spectrum of song into regular interactions with the babies.

Repertoire

The selection of repertoire became a focus of the project. The researchers discovered that practitioners knew a number of songs but their repertoire contained very few lullabies or quieter, slower songs. The project team encouraged the daycare staff to reflect on why they chose particular songs to sing and the purposes behind their singing. Their reflections revealed that most of the songs were lively, upbeat play songs and accompanied by actions. The practitioners typically explained the purpose of singing was to support language development, to encourage babies and toddlers to join in, particularly with actions, and to create a fun and lively atmosphere. The project team found that practitioners were sometimes conflicted in their realisation that babies also needed quiet, closeness and stillness. Encouraging practitioners to understand the value of stillness and to introduce songs to create a calm atmosphere and to soothe became one key purpose of the project.

The project arrived at a number of strategies for vocalising and singing with babies listed below (Ragdoll Foundation, 2017, p. 9).

- Develop an alertness to the baby's waking state, and look for every opportunity to engage with babies using vocal styles from the *Spectrum of Song*.
- Listen out for and imitate any of the baby's vocalisations. Exaggerate, repeat, make bolder. Leave space for the baby's responses. Create a 'musical dialogue'.
- Take turns to make up a sound, copy and 'play' with it. Change it slightly each time in a kind of 'sound ping pong'.
- Mirror the baby's actions and add some matching sounds.
- Mirror the baby's utterances or vocalisations (for example, a yawn) and add actions and gestures.
- Play with sounds. Use exclamations such as 'Ouch!' or 'Yippee!' or 'No!' or 'Yay!' or 'Ugh!'; Repeat in a playful way. Exaggerate the pitch/volume/tempo.
- Convert instructions or suggestions into 'singese'. For example, 'Let's go and get some lunch'; or 'shall we change your nappy?' Repeat and make into a kind of chant or chorus.
- Convert songs: for example, turn play songs into lullabies.
- Enjoy precious moments of closeness and stillness with babies in your care and hum or coo very quietly.

Spontaneous Play with Educational Percussion

As a new lecturer at the Froebel Institute, London in 1993 I was influenced by Froebelian philosophy and principles and initiated a research project that explored children's self-initiated play with educational percussion (Young, 2003). This project also drew on the work of Chris Athey who had incorporated theoretical ideas from Piaget, primarily schema theory (see p. 97), into a Froebelian, play-centred approach. I provided certain instruments that I thought would have play potential for 3- and 4-year-olds, echoing Froebel's interest in offering resources that would stimulate play in certain educational directions. The approach embraced Froebel's holistic philosophy to learning in that I was interested in how children played with the instruments multi-modally, using all their capacities. Through playing with the instruments children could simultaneously explore and also represent:

- qualities of sound – tone, timbre, pitch, volume
- musical patterning and structure, generated by their own movement vocabulary in interaction with the potentials of the instruments
- forms of musical knowledge such as simple melodic structures, rhythms, dynamics, phrasing
- creative expression through body movement, voice and expressive communications with a partner, and
- musical experiences from their own lives (e.g. imitate the playing movements of kit drum players in pop groups).

I studied how the structure of the play object – an educational percussion instrument – stimulates and channels certain forms of exploratory play. A 4-year-old presented with an Orff alto xylophone and offered one beater, may explore a number of different actions suggested by the structure of the xylophone. She may scrub the beater from side to side, tap each bar from the bottom to the top, tap the two wooden ends of the xylophone or strike the keys with energy and exuberance to produce a welter of sound. If analysed only in terms of musical criteria, asking the question in what way does the child's play demonstrate musical elements, the child's playing would seem to be random, messing about. If analysed in terms of action patterns, the forms of logic start to reveal themselves. So the child may scrub, tap individual notes and then start to form patterns made up of action groupings. For example, they may tap every note from the bottom to the top, then tap the very top, the very bottom in sequence, and then tap all the way down again. They may swish back and forth several times on the keys to produce a glissando sound and then wave the beater in the air with a similar movement pattern, return to the swishing and alternate the two actions – one sounding and one silent. Thus what may seem like random, unintentional playing starts to reveal intentional patterns based on structures of actions – schema as Chris Athey would have termed them – in interaction with the possibilities for action offered by the xylophone. In this way children are developing understandings of the relationships between their actions and the instrument they are playing, and the sounds they create. They organise and structure their sounding actions that form the basis of their own, self-generated music-making.

As the research project progressed it became clear that the presence of an interested, listening adult contributed to how the children's play progressed and so I began to focus my research interests on the role of the adult as play partner. Following a simple protocol of watching, listening and then joining in by copying the playing actions of the child, improvisations would progress and emerge in partnership. I then theorised the play partnering, drawing on theories of adult-infant interaction (see p. 149).

This approach to music play pedagogy, with its roots in Froebelian philosophy and the work of Chris Athey, a Froebelian influenced educator, has become widely adopted in early childhood music education practice in the UK.

Key Text

Susan Young. (2003). *Music with the Under Fours*. London: Routledge.

Comments and Connections

Froebel's original writings are often difficult to understand and covered many topics. However, the teacher training institutions established to disseminate the principles of his pedagogy have had a major and continuing influence on early childhood education philosophy and practice. Froebel's ideas are continually being reinterpreted to bring them in line with contemporary society and its education. Many of the kindergarten activities introduced by Froebel have endured over time: play with different sized blocks, occupations such as cutting, lacing and weaving, play in outdoor spaces with natural materials and songs and rhymes with actions. Some aspects of his beliefs about spirituality may have faded from contemporary educational thinking, but his fundamental conviction that the child should be viewed holistically remains.

The Froebelian image of childhood is one of children being treasured, loved and allowed freedom to play, although within some constraints. Some might, however, argue that this idealised image of innocence can result in children being disempowered and not allowed sufficient independence and agency. However Froebel's image of childhood needs to be understood within its historical context and in light of his aim to reform the education of young children by challenging the dominant conception of childhood at that time.

The value which Froebel placed on singing within the upbringing of the very youngest children and its importance in creating a close emotional bond between caring adult and baby has been borne out by recent research (see p. 151) and perpetuated in recent professional development projects. Interest in infant-direct speech and infant-directed singing have revealed their key contribution to early infant-adult interaction and thus their contribution to early development. His emphasis on finger plays with songs and rhymes has continued to be a plank of early childhood practice, especially with babies and toddlers.

Bibliography

Bruce, T., Elfer, P., Powell, S. and Werth, L. (2019). *The Routledge Handbook of Froebel and Early Childhood Practice*. Abingdon: Routledge.

Lilley, I. M. (1967). *Friedrich Froebel: A selection from his writings by Irene M. Lilley.* Cambridge: Cambridge University Press.
Ragdoll Foundation. (2017). *Babysong Booklet.* Banbury: Ragdoll Foundation. Retrieved from www.ragdollfoundation.org.uk/wp-content/uploads/2017/01/BabysongBooklet_CCCU_Feb2017.pdf.
Tovey, H. (2017). *Bringing the Froebel Approach to your Early Years Practice*, 2nd edition. London: David Fulton.

4 John Dewey: Learning through Experience

> I believe that education ... is a process of living, not a preparation for future living.
>
> (Dewey, 1897)

This quote by Dewey conveys the essence of his educational philosophy; that education is life itself. Transferring that idea into music education, music for children should always be a living activity, meaningful in the moment. Dewey, an American, was an eminent educationalist and philosopher whose work has had a significant influence on educational practice. His career was long and he wrote prolifically on philosophy, education and politics; always thinking about how education could be improved. His writing has been interpreted and re-interpreted by many scholars who have followed him and his philosophy continues to have relevance and influence today.

He did not, however, formulate a specific educational method and certainly did not write about music education although he valued music as a subject area in education. While at Chicago he established a laboratory school with his wife, Alice Chapman, where his educational ideas could be put into practice. At that school Eleanor Smith was employed to teach music and, being a close colleague of Dewey, interpreted his philosophy in her approach to music education.

John Dewey (1859–1952)

John Dewey was born in Vermont, USA in 1859. After graduating from university, he taught in schools for a few years before completing a PhD in psychology. He then took up university positions, first Michigan, then Chicago (1894 to 1904) and finally Columbia where he remained for the rest of his career.

Philosophy

During Dewey's long lifetime America changed dramatically and the social changes and tensions caused Dewey to consider the role of education within a changing society. He promoted the view that children learn through real-life experience in an active, child-centred way that is not separated from life itself. Schools, he argued, should not be places where children are passive recipients of schooling. Both teachers and parents should encourage children to be independent thinkers and nurture their curiosity.

Dewey belonged to the American school of pragmatism in philosophy. Pragmatism is based on the principle that the usefulness and practicality of ideas, values and policies is what matters. There is no absolute truth, only beliefs that have passed the test of contributing to the good of everyone.

Children, Dewey advocated, were to be guided by well-trained teachers. He believed that learning subjects – to be precise, learning the structure of a subject – encourages intellectual development. Thus the teacher's aim is to understand both the subject they are teaching and the needs of the child and then to provide learning experiences that weave the two together, enabling the child to discover the subject. So, Eleanor Smith, for example, encouraged the children to improvise song phrases and then guided them into making up new songs, based on the children's ideas but also drawing on her skills as a composer.

For Dewey cooperative learning was important in fostering the value of democracy among children; a value that would underpin a just and humane society. The most important task of schools was not to impart knowledge, but to teach the essential relationships between knowledge and wider social experience. He was critical of abstract, formal knowledge that had no relationship to real lived experience. In contrast to repetition and rote learning, he proposed a method of 'directed living' in which children would participate in real-world, practical workshop activities that would provide them with opportunities to think for themselves.

John Dewey is often cited as the philosophical founder of a theoretical view of education broadly termed 'constructivism'. Simply put, children construct their own understanding of new information by building on their previous knowledge and experience. The new information that they are encountering is matched against existing knowledge and children construct new or adapted understandings to make sense of the world around them. In such a theory of learning the teacher cannot control the children's learning for every child is making their own version. Beneath this theory of education is the philosophical idea that there is no absolute, fixed version of knowledge and every child creates their own interpretation.

While he emphasised that every child is an individual learner who brings their own history with them to their learning he also recognised the importance of learning in a group, learning from others and from others who are unlike you. That is the essence of a democracy, that there are many different voices and opinions, and children learn by listening to and considering different perspectives. For Dewey democracy did not refer merely to political processes, but rather referred to the dynamic, everyday processes of participation and equality. In this sense, music is a democratic art form that invites children to join in, on equal terms, and to contribute and coordinate their individual music-making to collective, unifying musical experiences.

Key Text

John Dewey. (1897). *My Pedagogic Creed.* Washington, DC: Progressive Education Association.

Principles

The key principles of Dewey's approach can be summarised as:

- discovery learning
- sensitivity to children's readiness for learning
- acceptance of individual differences
- learners constructing knowledge for themselves
- learning related to real-world contexts, and
- learning as a democratic process.

Dewey's Stages

From his experiences of working with young children in the laboratory school Dewey proposed some broad stages of development. An early stage is dominated by children's imagination and is emotionally charged and vibrant. This stage is characterised by free activity in which children make connections between many dimensions of experience. It then merges into a more experimental stage which is combined with reflective thinking. Dewey noticed that children's interests are highly personal and rooted in what is familiar to them.

'Wholes'

Dewey stressed the importance of 'wholes'; whole stories, whole songs and complete pieces of music. These whole forms then offer structure and framing for further activities that may focus in on detail – to support children's learning – but should always return to the whole song or piece of music.

Art as Experience

Dewey did not write specifically about music education, but he did write about the arts more generally in his book *Art as Experience* (1934). All art, including music, he believed is an integral part of everyday life and is not so much a 'thing' as an experience. The value of music is what it is used for. Therefore we should not ask 'what is music?' but 'when is music?'. So, to interpret Dewey, the difference between listening to and appreciating the sounds of nature, or a baby tapping a spoon on the table, listening to popular music at home and listening to classical Western art music in a concert hall is only one of interpretation, not anything intrinsically more or less valuable within the sounds/music *per se*. They can all be musical experiences within certain contexts. They can all be 'when music' is being made. It is the social and cultural context which bestows those distinctions on the music; and gives it those values. This idea might be contentious with some who would claim that music contains enduring, intrinsic values which can be detached from context.

What follows from the 'when is music?' question is that music cannot be treated as if it exists in a vacuum, isolated from the world. If it is not isolated from the world, then it is also not isolated from all the world's issues and problems. This idea connects with calls to recognise the gender, class, racial and other biases that exist in the practices of music. It asks music educators to be alert to issues of freedom, inclusivity, social responsibility and social justice in music education.

Moreover for Dewey artistic experience is a vital form of experience in which some things come together and crystallise. For Dewey artistic experience can offer moments of insight when educators with children can encourage them to think and talk about what is important in the world. This was a radical call for educational and political empowerment through art, importantly beginning with children's close involvement in their own musical experiences and music of their own making, rather than the more distant and detached art music that is the music of experts and elites.

Music was a valued part of Dewey's laboratory school where it was viewed as a mode of communication and expression. The commonest activity was singing, with a special emphasis on children developing their individual creativity through song composition. At that time creative activities received little attention in music education. In contrast, for Dewey and Eleanor Smith, children making their own music was viewed as a means of musical expression that could support the development of expressive abilities in all areas of life.

Image of Childhood

Dewey viewed children as capable, active and autonomous learners (Dewey, 1897). He emphasised children's existing competences and their potential for learning. While he advocated active, play-based learning that would build on children's natural curiosity and exploration, he also wanted children to be empowered with skills and formal knowledge – such as the knowledge and skills of music as a subject – that would enable them to adapt to new situations.

The Philosophy in Practice

Eleanor Smith (1858–1942) was a composer and music educator living in Chicago whose work captured the interest of Dewey. She had founded the

Hull House Music School in Chicago where she applied her progressive teaching ideas. She was later invited to contribute to the work of the laboratory school established by Dewey and his wife at Chicago University. Early in her career she had studied voice and composition in Germany and had encountered the educational philosophy of Friedrich Froebel. Drawing on Froebel's ideas Smith proposed that children should be allowed to learn intuitively by participating actively in singing and other musical experiences. This intuitive, participatory approach was in contrast to the learning of music through dull drill and memorisation that was the usual method at the time. In the activity described below, the children are working collaboratively, sharing improvised phrases to contribute to one final version of a song under the teacher's guidance. In keeping with Dewey's ideas, she recognised that the teacher plays a crucial role in supporting and guiding children's learning. The activity becomes an opportunity to introduce musical knowledge such a pitch and melodic line, but within a 'whole song' activity which is based on the children's musical inputs and is meaningful for them.

> Influenced by Dewey's ideas, Eleanor Smith promoted a creative musical activity based on the group composition of songs. Simple phrases were improvised by the younger children and harmonized by the teacher. The older children would suggest melodies and other class members would make suggestions. As the children commented on the melody and how it might be developed, terms such as pitch, tone, melodic line could be introduced and be applied meaningfully in musical contexts.
> (School record, October 21, 1898; held in Milbank Memorial Library archive)

In addition Eleanor Smith wrote several books of songs for children. Singing she wrote, is the foundation on which school music is built. She stressed the importance of young children singing with beautiful tone and of artistic presentation and interpretation to convey the spirit of the song. She was perhaps the first to compose songs which were adapted for young children both to suit their vocal abilities and to be musically appropriate and engaging for them. Many songs, for example, incorporated movement and playful actions. A song about a windmill included a phrase of accompaniment when children stopped singing and moved like windmills. In *Songs for a Little Child's Day* she explained what she considered to be the compositional characteristics of songs for children (Smith, 1910, pp. v–vi):

- Form. Short and compact, with short phrases that do not require long breath control which would be difficult for young children.
- Melodies. The melodies should seldom move outside the eight tones of the major scale. The pitch of the child-voice must be taken into account.
- Intervals. Difficult intervals should be avoided.
- Rhythm. Over-complicated rhythms are to be avoided.

- Accents. A large proportion of strongly accented tunes will be appropriate to the stage of development of the little child, although too many such tunes will result in over-stimulation.
- Sense of pitch. The imitation of natural and mechanical objects in the songs can help to establish the sense of pitch.
- Piano accompaniments. A well-constructed accompaniment develops the ear and musical taste. But children should master the melody before they sing to accompaniments.
- Above all, a great affection and sympathy for children and a thorough understanding of their musical needs and limitations must dominate the work of the artist.

She was also concerned with social issues of the day and some of her songs reflect these concerns. Her songs continued to be published in song texts for children for many years. Her image of musical childhood was of simplicity but with concern not to compromise musically, but to ensure, as she says, grace and beauty.

> Songs for little children, to serve their purpose fittingly, should express the simplicity of childhood, should embody its moods and reveal its charm. And while simplicity is perhaps the first quality which urges its claims upon teacher and composer, variety and beauty of form are not less important. The simple may not be the commonplace, the monotonous, the vapid. The tiniest melody must have some measure of grace and beauty if it be reckoned worthy to train the musical sense and develop the taste of young children.
>
> (Smith, 1910, p. v)

Key Text

Eleanor Smith. (1910). *Songs for a Little Child's Day*. Springfield, MA: Milton Bradley Company.

Comments and Connections

Many progressive educational movements which emerged in the first half of the twentieth century were influenced by Dewey. Dewey, in turn, endorsed principles set out by Froebel: that the source of learning should be the self-generated activities of the child; that the goal of education should be the social, co-operative development of the child and finally that cooperative living in the school should reproduce, at the child's level, the larger society (in a democratic and ideal version) which children would enter.

He was critical, however, of Froebel's ideas of the natural unfolding of a child's learning suggesting it was too vague. In contrast, Dewey's constructivist view of learning anticipated the ideas of Piaget, Bruner and Vygotsky. As with Piaget he placed importance on active experience in the environment and as with many theorists, he saw the teacher as having a facilitative role in guiding children's learning and introducing the knowledge and structure of a subject. He was less concerned than Piaget, however, to define models of development that applied uniformly to all children, seeing each child as a unique individual. Dewey's educational philosophy, in paying particular attention to the social and community contexts of children's lives and learning, heralded Vygotsky's sociocultural theory.

Dewey mirrored Dalcroze in his recognition of the importance of holistic activity; the direct embodied experience from which more formal learning could be abstracted. So, for example, intuitive understanding of musical elements, such as pitch and rhythm, and skills, such as early notation reading, could be abstracted from the activity of singing songs that were emotionally satisfying and engaging to young children. This was the approach put into practice by Eleanor Smith. Her work was, however, focussed on songs and singing with movements and play actions to accompany the songs, rather than the freer bodily movement of Dalcroze. In specifying the musical characteristics of songs to ensure that they were suitable for young children's voices, she heralded the music pedagogy of Kodály and his followers.

The underlying theoretical basis of Dewey's proposal for a more child-centred approach, reflected in progressive education, has been criticised on the basis that children need, indeed, deserve to learn traditional subjects and their content, and to appreciate the cultural heritage that is passed from generation to generation. However this criticism misinterprets Dewey's pedagogical theory. While he condemned an early childhood education which ignores the experience of the child, at the same time he did not think that education should ignore formal, subject-centred knowledge. He pointed out that there was often no obvious connection between the play interests and activities of the child and the content of subjects to be learnt – no obvious connection between, say, a child's vocal play and improvised song singing and learning about pitch and melodic line. There is a conceptual gap. The central role of the teacher, therefore, is to bridge that gap. The teacher needs to identify those interests and activities which, with appropriate intervention, can be linked with more formal knowledge. Teachers unite their knowledge of the child and knowledge of the subject, using their pedagogical skills to find the points of connection.

Bibliography

Alper, C.D. (1980). The early childhood song books of Eleanor Smith: Their affinity with the philosophy of Friedrich Froebel. *Journal of Research in Music Education*, 28(2), 111–118.

Dewey, J. (1897). *My Pedagogic Creed*. Washington, DC: Progressive Education Association.
Dewey, J. (1934). *Art as Experience*. New York: Capricorn Books.
Smith, E. (1910). *Songs for a Little Child's Day*. Springfield, MA: Milton Bradley Company.

5 Maria Montessori: An Environment for Guided Learning

> The Silent Game: One day I had the idea of using silence to test the children's keenness of hearing, so I thought of calling them by name, in a low whisper ... this exercise in patient waiting demanded a patience that I thought impossible.
>
> (Montessori, 1936, p. 123)

Maria Montessori was an Italian educator whose philosophy of education was based on respect for a child's natural intellectual, physical and social development and on providing children with freedom to learn through play – but within prescribed limits. A cornerstone of the Montessori approach is to help the child to be as independent as possible in the belief that children are motivated to educate themselves, and can do so if the environment is enabling. Children are encouraged to select their own activities, to find the materials they need and to develop those activities, independently, for extended periods of time.

Living in the first half of the twentieth century and experiencing the tragedies of war her educational ideas extended beyond positive development for individual children to wider aspirations for global peace and social harmony.

The Montessori method has a long history of valuing and including music. Although Montessori did not consider herself a music educator, she worked with two colleagues – Anna Maccheroni and Elise Braun Barnett – who contributed their music expertise. Maccheroni helped to develop the music materials that are distinctive to the Montessori method.

Maria Montessori (1870–1952)

Maria Montessori had qualified as a doctor, the first female in Italy to do so, and at first worked with children who had special needs, becoming very interested in how they might be supported to learn. In 1907 she started working with children in a housing project located in a slum district of Rome. There she set up her first *casa dei bambini* (children's house) for 3- to 7-year-olds. She continued to develop her interest in children's learning and started to evolve a distinctive pedagogy based on what she described as a scientific approach of experimentation and observation.

DOI: 10.4324/9781003331193-8

Her work began with practice and from this her theories evolved. She observed the children carefully and then identified where learning potential could be developed and maximised by providing carefully designed materials and educational experiences. An important year was 1912 when her book, *The Montessori Method* was translated into English and the Montessori Society was formed in England. From then on, interest in her educational ideas spread rapidly to many countries.

Principles

Montessori's philosophy of education proposes that young children:

- think differently from adults
- learn from interactions with teaching materials
- learn best from teachers whose role is mostly to observe, to respond to the children's actions and to respect the children's own learning goals, and
- should be supported to become independent.

Self-education

Self-education, the idea that children are able to educate themselves, with independence, is one of the most important beliefs in the Montessori method. Children have an innate motivation to learn and Montessori teachers provide the environment, the inspiration, the guidance and the encouragement for children to self-educate.

Planes of Development

For Montessori, children developed through a series of 6-year periods termed 'planes' (0–6, 6–12, 12–18). These planes form a staged model that have similarities with other staged models such as Piaget's four stages of cognitive development (see p. 97). During each period, or plane, she proposed that children were sensitised to a particular kind of learning.

Absorbent Mind

The earliest plane, 'absorbent mind', separates further into two phases. The phase from birth to 3 years she termed the 'unconscious absorbent mind' and children then moved from age 3 years to 6 years into a 'conscious absorbent mind' phase. In the unconscious absorbent phase the child's mind absorbs directly from the environment. Between 3 to 6 years of age children begin to direct their conscious attention and to gather information deliberately from their immediate environment through sensory experience and physical interactions.

Conscious Mind

The second plane encompasses the age phase 6 to 12 years. The absorbent mind shifts to become the conscious mind. Learning now is deeper and slower, with children drawn less to simple repetition and more interested in variation and how things change. In this phase she suggests they are no longer solitary, they are more interested in working with their peers on activities that are mutually interesting. This is viewed as a particularly sensitive age phase for children's imagination and their ability to see creative possibilities in their experiences. At the same time their ability to reason is developing rapidly.

The Prepared Environment

Of central importance in the Montessori approach is the organisation of the environment. The environment is designed to support children's intellectual, physical and emotional development by encouraging active exploration, choice and independent learning. The aim is to provide an environment that helps children strengthen their natural ability to concentrate and to lose themselves in their activities, with as much repetition as they want.

In addition the environment should be aesthetically pleasing and filled with easily accessible and specially designed learning materials. These materials isolate just one property intended to capture and focus the child's sensory attention as they explore. There are some materials specifically for music, for example, which direct the children's attention to properties such as pitch and timbre. The materials are designed to:

- be developmentally appropriate
- isolate properties
- stimulate activity
- appeal to children
- facilitate self-directed learning
- support continuity – by allowing the children to progress individually, moving from simple objects to more complex at their own pace, and
- support group interaction among children of older ages.

The equipment is also intended to develop the child's manipulative skills because they require the control and coordination of body, hand and eye.

The teacher's role with respect to the materials is to allow the children to explore, leaving them to be as independent as possible but observing carefully. Although the children have freedom to select what they do, this freedom is not unlimited. The teacher should intervene if children are finding it difficult to settle or to select what they want. Alternatively they may intervene if they consider the child needs to be guided towards the learning objectives inherent in the materials.

The Curve of Work

A central principle of the Montessori classroom is that children are allowed plenty of time to learn at their own pace and need uninterrupted opportunities to explore. Typically the schedule allows for periods of up to 3 hours of exploration when children are free to pursue their own interests, ideally without adult intervention. There is an expectation that children may take a while to settle into a meaningful activity and that they usually follow a similar pattern known as the 'curve of work'. They may not at first settle on one task but may flit from activity to activity. After this first explorative phase they may become involved in something and focus, but this phase may be more active and noisy. Finally if the high activity phase continues children may move into a final phase where there is greater focus and the most valuable learning takes place.

The allocation of long periods of time for exploration and the carefully structured environment may give the impression of a slow pace and rather orderly way in which learning is managed. However Montessori educators believe that when children are engrossed in an activity, they are likely to be making important conceptual links and developing a deep understanding. They aim to create these conditions and then allow such moments to continue, observing carefully.

The Centrality of Observation

Observation is central to the Montessori approach. The 'wisdom of the educator', claimed Montessori, comes from observation and close contact with the child's intellectual, physical and spiritual development. Montessori was among the first to try to establish a science of observation and to recommend that educators should be trained in methods of observation.

There are three stages to observation.

1. To watch and gather information, 'in the moment', objectively, without bias or allowing prior experiences to influence.
2. To reflect on the information gathered and to arrive at conclusions.
3. To put a response into action.

The Montessori approach places emphasis on the educator understanding children as individuals with individual dispositions and capabilities while simultaneously being aware of their developmental stage. The aim is to try to understand children's intentions and ideally not intervene, or intervene minimally, to help them to work things out for themselves, not to direct or instruct them.

Parents as First Educators

Montessori saw parents as crucial and described them as the first educator. She stressed the importance of forming good relationships with parents in order to create the triangle of child, parent and educator.

Image of Childhood

The Montessori approach is founded on a holistic image of children which integrates the intellectual, spiritual and emotional dimensions of their experiences. According to her view, the spiritual and natural laws of childhood development work together in the child's growth and education. Thus she describes the baby when born as a 'spiritual embryo', a phase which continues until 3 years of age. By this she means that babies and very young children require the care of an adult for their physical needs, but they have an inner, spiritual force, for the person they will become as they mature. Children should, therefore, be respected as individuals and educated in an environment that allows them to follow their own motivations and needs.

Key Text

Maria Montessori. (1936). *The Secret of Childhood.* (trans. B. Carter). New York: Longmans, Green & Co.

The Philosophy in Practice

From her observations, Montessori identified sensitive periods in which the child is predisposed to learning certain skills relating to many areas such as movement, language, social aspects – including music. She proposed that the period between the ages of 2 and 6 years is a sensitive period for musical development. Interest in music clearly continues after the age of 6 years, but she suggested that during this sensitive period children's ability to develop basic musical skills such as singing in tune and moving rhythmically is at its peak. This is when children begin to acquire a sense of pitch, melody and rhythm. The Montessori emphasis on education of and through the senses means that listening and developing aural skills are a priority.

Montessori music pedagogy is based on these principles.

- Music learning begins with listening and lessons in silence.
- Special music materials such as the Montessori Bells encourage auditory discrimination and problem solving.
- Listening to music and moving to music are important. Performed music (recorded or live) is played to encourage children to move spontaneously to the music.
- For older children, the first steps of learning notation are introduced via specially designed equipment.

Elise Braun Barnett, who worked with Montessori, compiled a book of piano pieces to be played by adults and intended for children to listen and move to (Barnett, 1973). The pieces are divided into categories that will encourage various types of locomotor movement such as marches, runs, gallops, skips, trots, slow walks, slow marches and waltz steps. The children are invited to respond first with spontaneous movements, then adjust their spontaneous movements to the music and then, finally, move with specific movements suggested by the teacher.

Music Materials

Music materials, also called manipulatives, encourage focused listening and listening to just one element of sound such as pitch or timbre. They are designed so that children develop their aural perception by learning to discriminate sounds and to compare, abstract and classify them. The children explore and handle the equipment independently, and so there is some integration of visual and kinaesthetic sensory experience with the aural experience. The materials and equipment should be beautiful and of good quality, in both appearance and sound.

The purpose of the music materials are to help a child to:

- sense single, isolated properties through actively manipulating the materials
- distinguish single properties from other properties
- absorb the sensory experiences
- abstract and internalise the properties from concrete experience
- compare, categorise, sort and classify properties, and
- name the property (with older children).

The Montessori Bells

This is probably the most well-known musical resource, often referred to as mushroom bells because of their shape. A complete set of bells standing on white bases includes the 8 pitches, middle C to an octave above. A complete set standing on brown bases includes the chromatic scale C to C.

Importantly, apart from the brown or white coloured bases, all the bells look exactly the same. Therefore the only property that distinguishes one bell from another bell is the pitch and the pitch is only identifiable by tapping and listening. Montessori therefore wanted the children to focus on listening and relying on their pitch-sense alone. With most instruments other properties such as size, shape or position in a row of keys gives clues as to pitch.

The Sound Boxes

These are six pairs of closed, identical cylinders containing different materials (e.g. sand to small stones) that vary in dynamic and timbre when shaken. The child must find the matching pairs. The only cue is the sound itself.

The Monochord

This looks like a small dulcimer with one string. The string can be seen vibrating and the child places their finger in different positions on the string to change the pitch.

Barbara Andress

Barbara Andress was an influential figure in early childhood music education in the US over a long period from the late 1960s. She was inspired by the Montessori method to create music environments equipped with didactic music materials, many of which she designed and initially made herself. She recommended setting up music play environments within nursery settings explaining that an adult-focussed session could not provide the play-centred learning opportunities that are the most suited to young children's ways of learning. For example she recommended providing a play area to promote children's free movement to music that included a means to play recorded music, mirrors for the children to watch themselves moving and props such as long ribbons to encourage certain types of movement.

Her suggestions for environments included what she referred to as a 'nook'. A nook was a small enclosure, large enough for children to crawl into and explore sound objects placed inside. A nook may also be constructed out of 'sound screens'; screens that had instruments fixed to one side. She also suggested a music circle, a designated area, marked out on the floor, where a teacher sits, ready to sing or music-play when children visit him, following the children's suggestions and requests.

> Andress describes how a small group of boys entered a sound box equipped with sandpaper blocks (fine to coarse sandpaper, producing differences in timbre and dynamic). She explains how the boys created a game of putting one of them, playing the role of baby, to sleep, singing an improvised 'go to sleep' song and playing the sandpaper blocks. The game was re-visited, extended and other children joined in.
>
> (Andress, 1980, pp. 92–93)

She especially liked to make music play mats for children to use while singing certain songs or listening to music. She created a scene on the play mat and the children would then tap characters on the mat to accompany the song or music.

> A play mat to be used with the song, 'Sally Go Round the Sun'. Andress suggests drawing a face on the child's right index finger. This finger is Sally, and she follows a pathway on the mat as the child sings the song. For the ending, the child uses a fist to pound on the stars shouting 'Ka-Boom'.
>
> (Andress, 1998, p. 73)

In her writing about music materials Andress affirmed Montessori's principles, adding to them by drawing on Piagetian theory. Her self-made equipment challenged children to make musical decisions, leading them to discriminate and classify sounds and guiding them towards certain learning objectives. Although inspired by the Montessori music materials she nevertheless considered they had certain limitations. In her view, they were less suitable for younger children and were over-focussed on pitch discrimination. The special instruments and music puzzles she made were designed to overcome those limitations.

Key Texts

Barbara Andress. (1980). *Music Experiences in Early Childhood.* New York: Holt Rinehart and Winston.
Barbara Andress. (1998). *Music for Young Children.* San Diego, CA: Harcourt Brace College Publishers.

Connections and Comments

Montessori's pedagogical ideas were rooted in a particular historical place and time. Her method has spread across the world with considerable variation in how it is implemented in different countries and in different schools. By promoting learning through play, Montessori was, in her time, at the vanguard of progressive approaches to early childhood education. Her holistic view of children and valuing of play reflected the views of earlier education philosophers, notably Froebel. Also in keeping with Froebel, Montessori's philosophy incorporated a strong belief in the spirituality of the young child. Her pedagogy is broadly constructivist in its conception in that children are considered to build their own knowledge and skills through experiencing the environment rather than passively absorbing the knowledge that an adult models or instructs them. Her belief that education can and should promote values of social harmony and peace continue to be highly relevant to contemporary educational practice.

Even though she achieved some radical and beneficial reforms through her work, there are some aspects which educators today might question. The approach has been criticised for being inflexible. Some say that although allowing for free play with materials, the approach is, nonetheless quite structured and directed by those materials and there is less room for free creative expression than her philosophy suggests.

Her conception of development as occurring in age related phases, or planes as she termed them, has been challenged by more recent ideas about development. She also implied that children are only interested in collaborating with their peers when they reach the age of 6 years and beyond. More recent research into young children's (even babies') interest and ability to interact with other children and adults would now refute that idea.

The approach of Émile Jaques-Dalcroze is mentioned in several of Montessori's books and his work had an influence on the movement activities that became part of the Montessori approach through the work of her colleague Elise Braun Barnett.

Bibliography

Andress, B. (1980). *Music Experiences in Early Childhood*. New York: Holt Rinehart and Winston.

Andress, B. (1998). *Music for Young Children*. San Diego, CA: Harcourt Brace College Publishers.

Barnett, E. B. (1973). *Montessori and Music: Rhythmic Activities for Young Children*. New York: Schocken Books.

Montessori, M. (1936). *The Secret of Childhood*. (trans. B. Carter). New York: Longmans, Green & Co.

6 Susan Isaacs: Freedom to Express

> It is the child's doing, the child's active social experience and his own thinking and talking that are the chief means of his education.
>
> (Isaacs, 1932, p. 65)

Susan Isaacs (1895–1948) is well known for having run the Malting House School in Cambridge, England from 1924 to 1927. The Malting House was a nursery school based on progressive educational ideas. Even though running the school represented only a short period in her career it was formative to her pedagogical theories. In her initial teacher training she had encountered the play-centred principles of Froebel and she was familiar with the theories of John Dewey that emphasised learning through active inquiry and facilitative teaching. Her experiences of working with young children at the Malting House enabled her to develop theoretical ideas of children's social, emotional and intellectual development which she explained in two key texts (Isaacs, 1930, 1932). These books were based on her detailed observations and reflections of individual children at the Malting House School.

She was very interested in psychoanalysis. She believed that experiences of infancy and early childhood shape our personalities and remain in the unconscious, which in turn, influences our learning. These ideas have gone out of favour in educational thinking which may explain why Susan Isaacs' work receives less attention today than it maybe deserves.

In the early years of the twentieth century progressive ideas were the preserve of private schools, such as the Malting House School, that catered for the children of a narrow social tranche of liberal-minded parents. By the 1950s – the period after the end of the Second World War – that situation had changed and progressive ideas were filtering into mainstream nursery and infant education. Susan Isaacs, through her positions in teacher training institutions, through her lecturing and through her authorship of texts for teachers in use during the 1930s to the 1960s, played a major role in that change.

In the 1950s the pedagogical ideas of Susan Isaacs were applied to music education by Eunice Bailey, who recorded her teaching experiences in a book published in 1958. Eunice Bailey's work influenced subsequent music educators, most notably John Paynter (see p. 140).

Susan Sutherland Isaacs (1885–1948)

In 1907, aged 22, Susan Isaacs enrolled to train as a teacher of young children at the University of Manchester. She went on to study philosophy, graduating in 1912 and in the next year studied for a masters degree in psychology at the University of Cambridge. She then held a series of lectureships before taking on the Malting House School. She entered psychoanalysis around 1920 and later trained to practise. She was, therefore, a trained teacher, philosopher, psychologist and a psychoanalyst. These different perspectives, combined, contributed to her deep understanding of young children.

In 1933, she became head of department in the newly formed Department of Child Development at the Institute of Education, University of London; a position that allowed her to promulgate her ideas widely among teachers and college of education staff.

Image of Childhood

Susan Isaacs' image of the child was a distinctive element of her practice. Like Froebel and Dewey before her she considered play to be children's work and believed children should be free to follow their own interests. However, in contrast to an image of young children as innocent and needing to be gently guided and protected (which is a common theme in early childhood education), there were few constraints imposed on the children at the Malting House. For example, children handled and dissected dead animals and climbed outdoors in ways that would be considered too risky nowadays. They could also express their emotions freely.

> Here the children's crudities, the disorder of their emotions, their savagery even, are allowed to show. Fights and squabbles often occur ...
> (Gardner, 1969, p. 65)

Isaacs believed in the importance of psychoanalysis to inform her study of young children. The children participated in role play involving strong, heroic characters and the expression of aggression because she believed this kind of play empowered the children and released anxieties and frustrations. In her view, emotional development was interdependent with cognitive development. She therefore tolerated children's expressions of emotion rather than try to repress them.

Principles

Susan Isaacs believed strongly that teachers must start with children and develop their pedagogical thinking from listening and observing.

Observation and Individualisation

At the Malting House School Susan Isaacs developed a method of observing and recording children's activities which she described as 'objective behaviouristic records' (Isaacs, 1930, 1933). She recorded the children's activities in naturalistic situations, emphasising the importance of first-hand, objective observations of individual children's behaviour and noting down exactly what they said (Isaacs, 1933, p. 18). The observations would reveal the 'natural foundation' of each child's understanding and acquisition of knowledge, as an individual. This method of observation grew directly from her background training in psychoanalysis. She was always curious to try to understand and interpret the children's unrestrained behaviours.

Holistic Development

Susan Isaacs considered children's development to be holistic, integrating social, emotional and intellectual development. All three dimensions of development are interdependent. By this she meant, for example, that emotions might motivate and guide the intellect just as the intellectual exploration might promote emotional development.

The Importance of Play

Susan Isaacs shared an emphasis on play-based learning with many other progressive educators. She viewed play as the context for children's problem solving activities, whether these were cognitive or emotional problems. She was especially interested in how the nursery environment could stimulate and enable children's play and also in how the adult facilitates problem-solving play.

Eurhythmics

Although Susan Isaacs' pedagogy was general and not focussed on music education, she was an accomplished musician and played the piano for children to move to, adopting approaches from Dalcroze eurhythmics which at that time was becoming more widely known in England. The school later employed a specialist teacher of eurhythmics. The only other mentions of music in her books, however, are of singing children's songs and playing records on a gramophone.

Key Texts

Susan Isaacs. (1930). *Intellectual Growth in Young Children*. London: Routledge.
Susan Isaacs. (1932). *The Children We Teach*. London: University of London Press.

The Theory in Practice

The little-known work of Eunice Bailey in the 1950s illustrates the educational theories of Susan Isaacs applied to music education practice. Bailey had worked first with children in a nursery, aged 3 years and above, and then in an infant school with 5- to 7-year-olds. She was well connected with the progressive infant movement that arose after the Second World War, led by lecturers at the Froebel Institute, London. She held a Susan Isaacs memorial scholarship awarded by the Institute in 1957 and we can therefore assume that she received this award in order to write about her interest in applying Isaacs' pedagogical ideas to music.

Eunice Bailey's book, published in 1958, contains many vivid descriptions of individual children's activity, including their talk, adopting a very similar approach to Isaacs' observational method. The book offers a highly personal, reflective account of experimental music practice. She was not trying to offer a prescriptive model for others to follow nor describing a series of successes but was, as the title states, 'discovering music with young children'. Her reflections and decisions about practice were, in keeping with this Isaacs' pedagogy, not generalised in relation to a group or class or age of children, but made specifically with respect to individual children. As Susan Isaacs had done before her, Eunice Bailey viewed children's self-initiated role play involving drama and dance with music as an opportunity to express their inner emotional lives and to deal with possible inner conflicts.

She took as her starting point children's improvisational play, with a particular emphasis on stories, drama, dance and various forms of role play.

> Six-year-old Ann danced into school singing this song one morning, round the classroom, along the corridor, round the hall, back to the classroom, out into the playground, round and round, until she had three more children singing and dancing with her. 'Where did you learn that song?' I asked her, when, quite breathless, they eventually subsided on mats in the book corner. 'I didn't learnt it, I thought it,' replied Ann, 'it just came – on the way to school. Isn't it a lovely one? Let's do it again.' And off they went, to end up in the hall, making up a dance to the little tune.
>
> (Bailey, 1958, p. 13)

Eunice Bailey's work was based on these principles.

- To provide an environment for self-expression and to encourage make-believe and imaginative play. Thinking and reasoning, she believed, emerge from fantasy (sic).
- To value artistic activity as a controlled outlet for emotions.
- To integrate movement, drama, free dance, story and music, initiated in play by the children, with particular emphasis on rhythmic movement.

Music is one interwoven dimension in an approach which values the integration of the arts.
- To offer young children opportunities to grow in social understanding and cooperation.
- To value close observation and the documentation of actions and speech.
- To identify children's interests as the starting point for introducing conventional music knowledge (e.g. knowledge about orchestral instruments, notation and listening to music on a gramophone).

Key Text

Eunice Bailey. (1958). *Discovering Music with Young Children*. London: Methuen and Co.

Comments and Connections

Susan Isaacs' work represents a continuity of Froebel's emphasis on play as the source of learning and Dewey's philosophy of education. She gave renewed impetus to the value of play – particularly imaginative play – in early childhood education from the 1920s onwards. Drawing inspiration from Isaacs' work, Eunice Bailey encouraged imaginative, free flow play and open-ended activity, without predetermined outcomes, as the basis for child-initiated musical activity. Eunice Bailey's work later influenced the early work of John Paynter and others, who, during the 1960s, developed the creative music movement (see p. 140). Teachers who adopt an Orff approach may also encourage mixed media activity combining song, story, drama, dance and role play, but improvised within a guiding framework and pre-given structure – rather than spontaneous, free and self-initiated as in the practice of Bailey.

Susan Isaacs demonstrated the importance of close observation and active listening to children, as had Montessori before her and the educators of Reggio Emilia who came later. She was concerned to understand children on their terms, to understand what was of deep concern to them, intellectually and emotionally. Eunice Bailey's text illustrates this observational approach applied to music. A more recent emphasis on 'tuning in' to babies and very young children in order to be musically responsive to them owes much to these earlier influences from psychoanalytic pedagogy.

Some of Susan Isaacs' theoretical ideas are contentious today, given her reliance on psychoanalytic theories of Melanie Klein and also her belief in the genetic inheritance of intelligence from Cyril Burt. After the 1950s, progressive education shifted to put developmental psychology as the theoretical basis of child-centred approaches rather than psychoanalytic theory. That shift may explain why interest in her work diminished.

Isaacs was well acquainted with the work of the Swiss psychologist Jean Piaget who visited the school in its early days and she was critical of some elements of his theory, specifically his reliance on fixed stages. However, her critique of Piaget's theory largely went unnoticed. Susan Isaacs always maintained that younger children simply lacked experience; they did not, as Piaget's theory implied, lack the ability to think logically at a young age. Her criticisms were more in line with thinking that came to the fore in the 1990s, and she heralded those revisions of cognitive development.

Bibliography

Bailey, E. (1958). *Discovering Music with Young Children*. London: Methuen and Co.
Gardner, D. E. M. (1969). *Susan Isaacs*. London: Methuen Educational.
Isaacs, S. (1930). *Intellectual Growth in Young Children*. London: Routledge.
Isaacs, S. (1932). *The Children We Teach*. London: University of London Press.
Isaacs, S. (1933). *Social Development in Young Children*. London: Routledge.

Part III

Many methods in music education have been designed but three have stood the test of time and are widely known. They are usually referred to by the names of their originators: Dalcroze, Orff and Kodály. All three originators were both composers and educators, and they all lived and worked in mid-European countries during the first half of the last century. Each developed a philosophy of music education with defined objectives and goals that arose from the times and places in which they were working.

These methods have strongly influenced the course of early childhood music education. In each section that follows I outline the underlying philosophy and principles and give illustrations of practice, although I do not go into the finer detail of content and techniques. There are many publications that offer further teaching ideas and materials. It is also important to recognise that the introduction of the methods into other countries by leading proponents, the setting up of training institutes and proliferation of courses has supported the continual development of each method, with variations in different countries.

The three approaches have much in common. First, each of these pioneers of music education perceived the need for change and their methods represented a reaction to what they viewed as weaknesses in music education at the time. They were founded on a belief in the importance of a quality music education for all children that would lay the foundations of future musicianship. All three shared an emphasis on rich musical experience before any kind of formal training or instruction. All aimed to train voice, body and ear as a basis for a musical education and to promote sensitivity and responsiveness to music through active participation. Their approaches assumed that all children could and should progress in learning music and move on to reading notation and learning to play an instrument. They are, at core, therefore, inclusive in their outlook.

Each method drew on techniques and teaching methods that were already in existence. This is often not appreciated. These include the use of solfa, bodily movement, rhythm chants using speech rhythms and syllables, and playing instruments designed for educational purposes. However, these music education innovators brought these techniques together in new

DOI: 10.4324/9781003331193-10

combinations, modified through their philosophies and through the musical materials which they composed for educational purpose. There can be a shorthand belief that Dalcroze focuses on movement, Kodály on singing and Orff on instruments. This is not strictly accurate, however, as each approach incorporates a synthesis of singing, moving and improvising with instruments, although with different emphases and styles.

Kodály first turned his attention to younger children, convinced that music education must start with the very young. Both Dalcroze and Orff originally developed their approaches with adults but then became increasingly involved in the education of young children.

All three philosophies for music education included wider aims for the benefit of a future society. Those aims included hopes for harmonious living, fostering of spirituality, preservation of national identity and of elite musical culture. While those aims may be less in tune with contemporary society, nevertheless these philosophies prompt us to review our own ideals for a future society that underpin music education.

Although each method has been around since the early to middle years of the last century, they have been developed and adapted by the many expert pedagogues who followed them; mainly women it should be said. They do not – and should not – remain static. Adaptation can, however, mean loss of the originating philosophy and principles, hence the importance of taking the time to grasp these. Adaptation also highlights the tension between the need to preserve the authenticity and integrity of an approach in contrast with the need be in tune with advances in educational thinking and with contemporary children's lives and social situations.

There have also been interconnections between the methods. The work of Jaques-Dalcroze preceded Kodály and Orff and both were directly influenced by his eurhythmics. Many contemporary music educators 'mix and match' by ensuring that they understand the principles of each method and then integrating them to suit their current teaching situations.

7 Émile Jaques-Dalcroze: Learning through Rhythmic Movement

> To be completely musical, a child should possess an ensemble of physical and spiritual resources and capacities, comprising, on the one hand, ear, voice and consciousness of sound, and on the other, the whole body (bone, muscle and nervous systems) and the consciousness of bodily rhythm.
>
> (Jaques-Dalcroze, 1921, p. 36)

In the 1890s, when he was a professor at the Geneva Conservatoire Switzerland, Émile Jaques-Dalcroze evolved a music education method which he initially called *rhythmic gymnastics*. In his rhythmic gymnastics the body became the first instrument of musical expression. Jaques-Dalcroze made his work known by giving lecture-demonstrations and publishing *La Méthode Jaques-Dalcroze* in 1906. Interest in his new method quickly spread across Europe and then further afield to Australia and the USA. A London school of Dalcroze eurhythmics, as the method was later called, opened in 1913 and ran until 1963.

The incorporation of rhythmic movement into early childhood music education was a gradual process. Educational philosophies were changing and the traditional approaches focused on singing by rote and reading notation were shifting to a more progressive view that included rhythmic movement as a means for the development of the whole child; body and mind as one. The kindergarten pedagogies of Froebel and later Montessori, the child-study philosophy and early psychology of Granville Stanley Hall, and the philosophy of John Dewey had all paved the way for the rise of interest in eurhythmics. The association of whole body movement with the development of rhythmic abilities, aural perception and musical understanding became an established idea, later incorporated into the methods of both Orff and Kodály.

Émile Jaques-Dalcroze (1865–1950)

Born in Switzerland, Jaques-Dalcroze studied composition, first at the Geneva Conservatoire of Music and then in Paris and Vienna. In 1892 he was appointed professor at the Geneva Conservatoire and in 1910 he founded a training college at Hellerau near Dresden, Germany. During the First World War Jaques-Dalcroze established his own school in Geneva, the Institut Jaques-Dalcroze, where he taught until shortly before his death. The Institut continues to this day as an international centre perpetuating his philosophy for music education.

Philosophy

Teaching at the Geneva Conservatoire Jaques-Dalcroze soon noticed that his students played technically but typically did not hear or feel the expressive character of the music that they were playing. He began to experiment with ways to improve his teaching. He would ask the students to move about, to feel the beat and the rhythmic character of the music and to conduct the metre of the music with large gestures. He then improvised at the piano and asked the students to respond in movements to the character of the music he played.

What had started as a method for conservatoire students soon expanded to the education of young children. The philosophy of eurhythmics is based on the idea that mind, body and emotions work as one and this unity is fundamental to learning in music. Jaques-Dalcroze wanted to create an approach to music education in which both sensory and intellectual, mind and body experiences, are fused. He wanted his students to be able to say not 'I know' but 'I feel', and for emotional expression to be core to their musicianship. Through rhythmic movement, he proposed, children would learn to think musically and have greater ability to concentrate, listen discerningly and coordinate physically.

He promoted the idea that music education should centre on active involvement in first-hand musical experiences not only through moving (for which his work is primarily known), but also through singing and performing. Active experience of music in which the whole body is infused with musical awareness must come before the techniques of reading notation or learning to play an instrument. He believed that music is, fundamentally, movement and that both rely on tension, relaxation, phrasing, symmetry and form. Rhythm, he proposed, is the foundation not just of music but of life itself. His philosophy grew to include a belief in the development of a more musical society through the holistic rhythmic education of all children.

The women (mainly women) who trained, took up and continued the approach, have added their own stamp. Drawing on the core philosophy, ways of teaching have developed and transformed in new educational, social and cultural environments. Many countries have their own history of Dalcroze work. In England Ethel Driver directed the professional training programme in London. She was followed by her sister Ann Driver who started the British Broadcasting Corporation's (BBC) Music and Movement broadcasts for schools in 1934 based on her adaptation of Dalcroze eurhythmics for radio. These radio lessons were very successful and continued until the 1960s.

It is interesting to note that for women in the early part of the last century, participating in eurhythmics was adventurous for its times. Students dressed in short sleeved tunics with bare legs and feet to allow for free movement. This went against conventional codes of dress and comportment for young women. There was a spirit of feminism among the women who were drawn to the work and promoted it.

Principles

The Dalcroze method combines three equally important components; eurhythmics, solfège and improvisation. These three components are interdependent and should be taught together so that they complement and reinforce one another, thus providing a complete musical education that blends creativity, movement and aural training. Many now replace the Dalcroze solfège based on a fixed do (which I explain in a later paragraph), with Kodály musicianship which is based on a moveable do (see p. 85).

Multiple Senses and Whole Body Learning

Dalcroze maintained that music should be experienced, taught and learnt through all the senses, in synchrony; the kinaesthetic, tactile, aural and visual senses. Moreover, the whole body, its core and larger muscles, should be infused with rhythmic awareness and musical expressivity, not just the smaller-muscle extremities of hands and feet.

Elements of Music

Children are introduced to the musical elements of pulse, rhythm, metre, dynamics, timbre, phrasing and form through direct experience, in movement primarily, but also through the voice and by improvising on instruments.

Starting with the Child's Own Movements

Young children have an individual body movement vocabulary which is determined by their size, coordination abilities, movement skills, their temperament and personality. Music learning and teaching should start with children's own body movements and the familiar movements they use in everyday life.

The adult usually initiates a movement idea – but allows freedom for the children to interpret the idea in movement in their own way. The educator then observes the children carefully and adds accompanying music (playing or singing), adjusting to the children's movement style, character and tempo. For this reason live music, sung or played, is preferable to recorded music because the music can be matched exactly to how the children are moving.

Movements are usually divided into non-locomotor (on the spot) or locomotor (movement through space).

- Non-locomotor: jump, stamp, stretch, curl, sway, bend, swing.
- Locomotor: walk, jog, run, leap, skip, gallop, hop, slither, crawl, roll.

Natural Tempo

Everyone has a natural tempo – also referred to as spontaneous motor tempo – at which they can best perform certain movements. Body shape, weight and size, health, personality and emotional state affect this natural tempo. Because of their smaller size and differently proportioned bodies children are likely to perform many movements at a faster pace than older children and adults will perform the same movements. The Dalcroze approach suggests that the young child's own movement vocabulary at their natural tempo should be the starting point for learning to keep in time with music.

It is a central principle of eurhythmics that the teacher matches the music to the children's movement tempo and style – rather than, vice versa, expecting young children to match movements modelled by the teacher or to match the beat of the music played in advance. Teaching strategies are carefully designed to enable children to achieve this match.

Eurhythmics teachers make a distinction between 'moving together' and 'moving to the beat' because the two skills have separate underlying mechanisms and developmental trajectories. Asking children to synchronise their movements with one another, as in ring games for example, may be a more achievable task than moving to the beat of given music.

Time, Space, Energy

In movements to music there are inter-relationships between the time, space and energy the movements require.

- Time: the tempo and duration.
- Space: the distance covered, the level and dimension (large or small).
- Energy: the energy or power used, the quality of the movement (heavy, light, accented).

Many typical activities in eurhythmics work with these relationships by asking children to adjust one dimension, the time span for example, and then to focus on how that affects the space and energy. Walking very slowly may require little energy and be easier with large steps that take up more space. Running requires more energy, the steps may be quicker, but also smaller, taking up less space.

Inhibition and Control/Incitation

Eurhythmics teachers will include quick response activities where a musical signal sung or played on an instrument asks the children to make a change. These activities might be as simple as stop and start games, or a change from one type of movement to another such as walk to run. The aim is to develop bodily control, coordination and responsiveness. The signals and responses become more complex and challenging. The educator observes the children and ramps up the challenge little by little. These activities ask the children to listen carefully, decide instantly and show they have understood through their movement responses.

Performing music and moving rhythmically both involve preparation (anacrusis), a moment of action (crusis) and then reaction and recovery (metacrusis). A single phrase of music and movement includes these elements. For example, children may be each standing in their own hoop on the floor, spaced out. They are asked to prepare to run to the next hoop for the duration of a musical phrase and arrive exactly as the phrase concludes. They listen, set off, judge the duration of their running pathway, arrive in the new hoop spot on time and recover.

Improvisation

Improvisation is central to eurhythmics. Children either improvise in movement to music or – vice versa – improvise music with voice or instrument to accompany movement. These kinds of activities are designed to increase children's ability to be musically expressive and also to become musically responsive to music they hear or movement they see.

Solfège and Ear-Training

Jaques-Dalcroze incorporated solfège into his method. This is a method of sight-singing and ear-training using the fixed do system that is common in parts of central Europe. According to this system do is always C. The sharps and flats to create the different scales are sung with altered solfège syllable sounds. Jaques-Dalcroze wrote materials for solfège designed to develop a sense of tonality and harmony; for Dalcroze this was a higher priority than developing music literacy and sight-singing skills.

Equipment

Equipment is sometimes used such as balls, scarves or short ropes that encourage certain types of movement and emphasise rhythmic qualities. Objects that mark out the floor such as hoops or straight sticks support the judgement of movements in space in relation to time and energy. Small hand-held drums are part of traditional eurhythmics exercises and are used to tap out rhythms. Nowadays these may be supplemented by a range of hand-held percussion that can be played while moving.

Image of Childhood

Children are viewed, holistically, as learning through body-mind unison and as needing the freedom to move and be active, creative and expressive. There is a suggestion of primitivism, recapitulation, in the idea that children should first engage with music through rhythm and bodily movement.

Key Text

Émile Jaques-Dalcroze. (1921). *Rhythm, Music and Education* (trans. H. F. Rubinstein). New York: G. P. Putnam's Sons.

The Method in Practice

Ideally the educator and children can work in a large open space that allows for free movement. They are dressed in clothing suitable for movement and have bare feet if the floor surface allows or, alternatively, wear soft shoes.

> *A class of 5-year-olds are invited to walk slowly as if carrying something with great care. The teacher watches as they move and picks up the average walking speed of the class and quality of their moving. She begins to improvise at the piano, quietly at first, so that her music matches their movements. She notices how almost all the class settle into a common tempo and move in synchrony, but also has an eye for a few who find it difficult to coordinate their movements in time. One child is so engrossed in an imaginative idea of carrying something cradled in both arms that she pauses the activity to ask what he is carrying. It's his new baby sister. 'Let's watch him carry baby and all try to copy exactly how he moves', she suggests.*
>
> *Next she stops playing. The children sit. She plays at a very slow tempo and invites individual children to walk in and out of the others, seated on the floor and asks them to 'make their feet step just the same as the music steps'. Children are invited to comment on whether the pace of feet and music is the same? Then all the class stand up to try and walk at this slow pace. The slow pace continues for a short while, then, as a surprise, she suddenly changes the tempo, playing at a fast pace and, laughing, the children adjust to brisk walking. The playing speeds up even more to become a run – then a sudden stops, silence, and back to slow.*

The teacher:

- starts with the children's own movements and introduces imaginative ideas to encourage a tempo and quality of moving

- observes and responds to the movement tempo and style of the children
- adds music to the children's movement so that they hear the music-movement connection
- picks up on what the children do, individually, and incorporates it as the lesson unfolds.
- selects an interesting movement quality from one child for all the children to imitate
- provides a musical stimulus for the children to match their movements, and
- extends the activity into quick movement responses to tempo changes in the music.

There should ideally be a give-and-take – a kind of music-movement dialogue – in which both the children and the adult are contributing ideas as the lesson unfolds. The educator, observing the children carefully judges how to introduce new challenges into the lesson in order to build on and extend the children's learning and skills.

The children are encouraged to listen attentively and to match their movements to what they hear, reacting to any changes that the educator may introduce. Usually striking changes are introduced at first, that may then become more subtle, thus training the children's responses and awareness both aurally and physically. The social dimension is emphasised through activities that encourage children to move with awareness of the whole group. Paired and small group work also support social interaction.

Key Text

Elsa Findlay. (1971). *Rhythm and Movement: Applications of Dalcroze eurhythmics*. Secaucus, NJ: Summy Birchard.

Comments and Connections

While the value of movement as a medium for learning in early childhood music education is now widely accepted, reflecting the broad influence of eurhythmics over many years, the underpinning philosophy and the more precise principles and pedagogical strategies of the Dalcroze approach are often less well known. In addition, the Dalcroze method is primarily thought of as a movement-based approach and not in its full tri-partite form of movement with vocal/aural training and improvisation. Moreover the more formal rhythmic movement activities of eurhythmics are better known than the movement improvisation. Plastique animé, as it was termed, is a dimension of the Dalcroze method which encourages free improvisation of movement to music. Freely improvised dance and dramatic movement can be part the eurhythmics approach and these movement styles are particularly valuable for younger children. Freer movement to music that starts to incorporate role play and dramatic narratives has similarities with the approach of Eunice Bailey.

In the original version of eurhythmics, the educator improvises, typically on piano but other instruments may also be played. However this pedagogical technique is less often observed because the educator needs to be skilled at improvising for children's movement. So one drawback of eurhythmics is that in its most complete and faithful application it calls for the ability to improvise on a melodic instrument.

Dalcroze emphasised an education of the senses and non-verbal, embodied experience and in this respect his work may appear to have similarities with Montessori's emphasis on sensory education. However, there is an important distinction. Montessori advised isolating the sensory experience so that children focus and attend to just one mode of perception, whereas Dalcroze recommended a synthetic approach in which sensory experience is integrated and holistic. Similarly, rhythmic movement in the Montessori method is offered within a framework of composed pieces which direct the children to certain pre-determined movements, rather than allowing the movements to be generated by the children's own movement vocabulary.

Both Kodály and Orff, who developed their approaches to music education later than Jaques-Dalcroze, were influenced by Dalcroze eurhythmics. Both incorporated principles of learning through bodily movement but interpreted those principles through the prism of their own philosophies for music education and pedagogical priorities. In both methods, the interest in children's singing games as a source for music education learning tends to lead to movement activities that are derived from the styles and movements of singing games. Smaller, body percussion movements typically involving the hands and feet are preferred in contrast to whole body movements. Dalcroze educators would argue that whole body movements, especially locomotor movements through space, enable children to respond to and express the energy and dynamic qualities of music in contrast to the smaller, more static movements of body percussion. There is also the proposition that large muscle movements leave a stronger imprint on kinaesthetic memory than small muscle movements.

As with many music education pedagogies, the method is less well developed in work with the under-3s. However Ruth Alperson (2012) has explained how the principles are well suited to working with toddlers because the Dalcroze teacher is trained to look for musical ideas that correspond with toddlers' emotions, energies and movement style. She has developed work with babies and toddlers and their accompanying adults.

> Through improvised music, the teacher tailors the music to reflect the two-year-old's 'world', and so to 'reach into' the child with music. When the music that is improvised by the teacher is 'right' for the children, the music 'speaks' to and within them: they can shake the rattles with the rattling quality they hear and feel in the music, they can run with the running

energy and tempo they feel in the music—they can be wholly with the music.

(Alperson, 2012)

Dalcroze appears to have anticipated many developments in theoretical understanding, especially among psychologists, of the link between bodily and sensory experience and music. He was working from a practical and philosophical basis, but psychologists have subsequently added theoretical insights. Geneva was the home of Piaget, and at the Dalcroze Institut teachers during the 1970s were well aware of Piagetian theory and theorised eurhythmics from the perspective of Piaget's theory of sensorimotor learning.

Bibliography

Alperson, R. (2012). *The gift of Dalcroze to the very young child*. 30th World Conference on Music Education Music Pædeia: From Ancient Greek Philosophers Toward Global Music Communities, International Society for Music Education (ISME), Thessaloniki, Greece, 16–20 July.

Driver, A. (1936). *Music and Movement*, 1st edition. Oxford: Oxford University Press.

Driver, E. (1951). *A Pathway to Dalcroze Eurhythmics*. London: T. Nelson and Sons.

Jaques-Dalcroze, É. (1921). *Rhythm, Music and Education*. London: The Riverside Press.

8 Carl Orff: The Unity of Dance, Music and Language

> It is this emphasis on improvisation which is at the heart of the Orff approach, improvisation in speech, in song, in movement, in instrumental play, and in the art of teaching as well.
>
> (Carley, 1977, p. 81)

The experimental creative activity that later became Orff Schulwerk (school work) originated in Germany during the 1920s. Carl Orff, a German composer, was influenced by the 'new dance' movement of the early twentieth century and by Dalcroze eurhythmics, and began to develop work that aimed for a synthesis of dance, music, song and poetic language. The focus was on rhythm and on musicians and dancers improvising collaboratively, combining and blending the art forms (Orff, 1973, p. 17).

By the 1950s Orff Schulwerk had become established in many European countries, particularly Austria and Germany. During the 1960s it continued to spread to English-speaking countries. In 1961 the Orff Institute was founded in Salzburg, Austria, becoming an important centre for developing and disseminating the approach.

Orff Schulwerk contributed to a major shift in music education that took place around the 1960s which emphasised children creating their own music, in contrast to re-creating the music of others. Dance and drama had been the first art forms to suggest that children should be expressing their own imaginative ideas through improvised dance and drama and thus break away from the dominance of children learning to reproduce and perform the ready-made work of others. Music was slower to follow this trend, given the apparent technical difficulties of making music with instruments.

Carl Orff (1895–1982)

Born in Munich, Bavaria, Orff was a composer with a strong interest in education. After serving in the army during the First World War he returned to his activities as a musician, working with theatre and opera companies.

In 1924 Orff founded a training centre for gymnastics and dance, the Günther School in Munich, in cooperation with Dorothee Günther, a gymnastics teacher. The aim of the school was to provide a place for musicians and dancers to work together to gain better understanding of each other's art forms through collaboration and especially through combined improvisation.

In 1948 after the Second World War, Orff was invited to adapt and develop his work for children in the form of radio broadcasts to German schools. Together with a colleague Gunild Keetman, Orff evolved what he referred to as 'elemental' music for children and the two of them developed educational materials. This work led to the publication of five basic volumes of Orff Schulwerk called *Musik für Kinder (Music for Children)* (Orff and Keetman, 1976).

Philosophy

The Orff approach is based on the belief that every child possesses musical imagination and creativity which can be released and extended through improvisation activities that combine singing, speaking, moving and playing. The approach is designed to nurture children's innate musicality in a developmental, holistic and active way by building on the chants, songs, drama and games of childhood. The activities seek to closely match the childhood world of phantasy and play. According to Orff, rhythm is the medium through which children can be led to explore music and learn about music because rhythm is fundamental to children's speech and movement. Orff considered that too often children were taught basic musical knowledge and skills in mechanical ways that neglected self-expression. He argued for a method in which children play and create music, performing and improvising before any formal learning is introduced.

Music, speech and movement activities in Orff Schulwerk constitute 'elemental' music as he termed it. According to Orff, elemental experiences provide spiritual nourishment to the child because he considered this to be a 'primeval' human need. Here he defines elemental:

> The Latin term 'elementarius' means 'belonging to the elements', to the origins, the beginnings, appropriate to first principles ... what is elemental music? [It] is never music alone; it is bound together with movement, dance and speech; it is a music that one must make himself, into which one is drawn in not as listener, but as participant. It is unsophisticated, knows no large forms or grand structures; instead it consists of small series forms, ostinatos, and small rondo forms. Elemental music is near the earth, natural, physical, to be learned and experienced by everyone, suitable to the child.
> (Orff, 1973, p. 5)

Image of Childhood

For Orff childhood was a time, set apart, when children were immersed in and explored their own childhood culture of songs, games and stories. The music of childhood, according to Orff, is primitive, close to the origins and the beginnings of music. He viewed the child as possessing an instinctive musicality and so needing freedom to express their musical individuality, to play and to create, particularly in social group play.

Principles

Educators who are inspired by Orff refer to their work as the Orff process or approach, avoiding the term method. The process includes these four components.

1. Exploration: discovering possibilities in sound and movement.
2. Imitation: developing foundation skills in rhythmic speech and body percussion, in rhythmic movement, in singing and in playing instruments (educational percussion).
3. Improvisation: extending the possibilities of the foundation skills by encouraging children to find new patterns and combinations.
4. Creation: using material from the previous phases and applying skills to create new small forms such question and answer, theme and variations, rondo, or making small musical dramas using speech or story lines.

The four stages increase in complexity and support children to become gradually more independent, musically. Through these components, creating, practising and performing provide the learning experiences from which understanding and knowledge emerge. Children are offered every type of musical experience, listening, creating, performing and analysing in a variety of ever-shifting media; speech, movement, song, instruments and listening. The media may be experienced alone or in combinations; for example, a song might be sung alone, or with movements or with instrumental accompaniment. The different media are considered interdependent and complementary. Rhythm and form unites them. Musical ideas and concepts are actively explored in these different media and forms of participation so that they gradually take form and consolidate.

Speech Rhythm

The natural rhythm of words, in chants and rhymes, is a springboard for developing rhythmic awareness and independence.

Dance/Body Movement

The Orff approach incorporates dance and movement with a particular emphasis on body percussion, often in interesting patterns and combinations. Movements include locomotor and non-locomotor movement and the use of time, space and energy in free and patterned forms, similar to the pedagogical strategies of eurhythmics.

Song

The first songs are usually pentatonic (based on the five-note scale). The first book of the Schulwerk begins with the interval of the falling minor third which both Orff and Kodály regarded as the first and natural melodic starting point for young children. Melodically the books progress through pentatonic to major scales and then modes.

Percussion

Improvising music – in particular improvising on educational percussion instruments – is a key feature of the Orff approach. Activities usually start with body percussion and then move on to playing a variety of unpitched percussion instruments and specially designed tuned percussion instruments known as Orff instruments. The tuned percussion instruments are typically used for providing drone and ostinato accompaniments for songs and for exploring short musical ideas and improvising.

Body Percussion

The four basic movements, or gestures are clapping, snapping fingers, slapping thighs and stamping feet. These are not the only body percussion movements, others can be invented. The body percussion actions can be combined in rhythm patterns, they may be performed alone, or as an accompaniment to speech, singing or instrumental playing.

Untuned Hand-Held Percussion

Many different types of small, hand-held percussion instruments are provided – maracas, claves, wood block, triangle, finger cymbals, suspended cymbal, tambourine and hand drums. There should be an emphasis, however on quality so that these instruments produce a pleasing sound. The original range of hand-held percussion from the 1960s and 1970s is now usually extended with percussion instruments that have become available for educational use in more recent years, many with roots in diverse musical traditions.

Pitched Instruments

With the help of Karl Maendler, Orff developed a special set of pitched educational percussion instruments. The barred Orff Instruments are unique to the Orff approach and their widespread presence in educational settings is a lasting legacy. They were designed to be the right size for children to play, easily portable and to produce a pleasing sound with a minimum of skill required. They are intended to be child-appropriate, but not 'childish' instruments.

The instruments were based on the Cameroon balafon, Indonesian gamelan and German glockenspiels. They include:

- three sizes of xylophone: bass, alto, soprano (wooden bars)
- three sizes of metallophone: bass, alto, soprano (resonant thick metal bars)
- two sizes of glockenspiel: soprano and alto (small, thin metal bars), and
- individual bass bars (each bar fixed onto a resonating box).

The bars supplied for each instrument are diatonic (major scale) starting with C and extending for an octave plus a sixth. Chromatic instruments are available, but are generally not used in the earlier stages of Orff Schulwerk.

The bars are removable and teachers may prepare instruments by removing bars to leave only those required for a certain activity. The preparation may, for example, leave only the five notes of the pentatonic scale, or the two or three notes required to play a drone or ostinato part, or to improvise accompaniments to songs.

Imitation and Echo activities

In the early stages of a session children are typically asked to imitate a given model in echo clapping activities or singing call and response songs. These may develop into structured improvising activities in which the whole group clap a rhythm, sing or play a short motif or phrase. Then each individual child inserts an improvised pattern, melody or phrase before the whole group returns to the unison motif.

Imitation is considered to be the starting point of improvisation. The children are given simple musical materials and then invited to explore and make up their own individual variations and versions based on these simple materials.

Improvisation

Most teachers take as their starting point the kind of controlled improvisation with percussion which is explained and illustrated in the Orff manuals. Improvisation can range from simple variations on short word rhythms or melodic patterning to the building of larger musical structures by introducing contrasting ideas. Pre-existing melodic materials, such as folk song, may be taken as a basis for improvisation and many teachers restrict the range of sounds in the earlier stages to pentatonic (five-note) scales.

Group Activities

Working together, successfully and with enjoyment, is central to the approach. Singing, playing and dancing in group work develops the ability to listen to others and to learn how to follow and keep in time with others. A larger group of children is usually divided into smaller groups, each with separate musical parts that combine as a whole.

The Orff Approach in Practice

Ideally the educator has access to a room large enough for movement and where the Orff instruments can be set out, ready for playing.

> *A class of 6-year-olds chant, in unison, 'ickle ockle blue bottle, fishes in the sea, if you want a partner just choose me!' The words are taken from a Scottish folk rhyme. The children are invited to suggest body percussion movements to add, stamping their feet, tapping their knees and clapping. The teacher points out that the stamping movement the children chose for the first phrase picks out the pulse, whereas the tapping and clapping movements match the rhythm of the words. The children have been learning the difference between pulse and rhythm.*
>
> *The teacher focuses on just the third line of the rhyme 'if you want a partner' and asks two children to improvise with that rhythm on an alto xylophone using two notes a fifth apart. Two children then take 'fishes in the sea' to improvise a melodic ostinato on 3 different pitches and two more children do the same with the first phrase, 'ickle ockle blue bottle'. As the melodic ostinati gradually accumulate, the teacher asks children to hum a tune for the words. Gradually they start to suggest melodic ideas and the teacher picks out what he hears, repeats it and a song emerges. The children decide to shout 'just choose me!' as the final line and reinforce the words with strong movement gestures and a drum beat.*
>
> *Next the instrumental players must teach their playing parts to new children and the singing and playing roles are swapped. The children suggest acting out the song as a ring game and, taking ideas from the children, the teacher supports them in creating the ring game. The teacher next suggests that some children may find it useful to make simple notations of their playing parts to help the new children to learn. Some make up their own notated versions.*

The teacher:

- introduces a short traditional children's chant for the children to learn by rote
- transfers the rhythmic patterning of the rhyme into improvised body movements that are then transferred to instrumental playing
- follows the sequence of voice to body to instrument
- sequences the activities to move through imitation, exploration and improvisation

- guides the exploration and improvisation and restricts the musical options (e.g. using 2 or 3 pitches on a xylophone, taking one line of the rhyme)
- values the process of learning through discovery more than a final product or performance
- describes, labels, prompts and questions both to encourage spontaneous creative thinking and to develop understanding and knowledge
- encourages the children to work collaboratively by teaching playing parts to one another and suggesting ideas for a song and game, and
- prompts them to convert their improvised instrumental ideas into simple notations.

Carl Orff and his colleagues did not publish specific guidelines for teaching. There are, however, some defined expectations underpinning the method. The example illustrates how the activity progresses from simple beginnings to more complex elaborations. It also illustrates how the session moves sequentially but also smoothly from one medium to the next, keeping all children active and involved. The educator has to be skilful in having a clear, overarching idea of how the activity may develop but, at the same time, allowing it to progress through the contributions of the children. Literacy (learning to read notation) progresses alongside the other activities and starts with children's own made notations. Importantly active musical experience should precede reading and writing sounds in notation.

Key Text

Jane Frazee. (1987). *Discovering Orff: A curriculum for music teachers*. New York: Schott.

Comments and Connections

Orff considered children's culture to be the primary source for music learning: songs, games, rhymes and speech forms. The first published materials were based on children's culture from Southern Germany where the first adaptations of Schulwerk for children took place. Kodály, similarly, considered folk repertoire, the songs and rhymes of childhood, to be the best source material for young children's musical education. With respect to both methods, their origins in a European regional folk music impart a distinctive musical character. With the changing demographic of school populations and music education priorities that are now concerned to introduce children to a diversity of musics, drawing on European traditional folk music as the source materials needs to be reconsidered. Indeed, many contemporary Orff teachers incorporate a wider variety of musics into their teaching.

The Orff approach is based on the idea that was common in 1920s educational thinking that children's development could be mapped onto the development of music in a progression from so-called primitive or elemental forms to more evolved music that was more complex and culturally advanced. Ethnomusicology – the study of music in diverse cultures – was in its early days and had started to make known music and dance forms from non-European locations. The barred percussion instruments that Orff incorporated into his method were based on instruments brought to Germany from Cameroon and Indonesia. Likewise the musical sources of traditional children's chants and rhymes were thought to be a window on the origins of music. This theory of development as recapitulation is now considered to be outdated. It assumes that folk music and music of other cultures represent stepping stones on the way to the pinnacles of musical achievement in the European classical tradition. For Orff his interest in non-European musics combined with his interest in Jaques-Dalcroze's blend of rhythm and movement convinced him that rhythm was the foundation of music. Rhythm, approached through the integration of dance and music forms was associated with what were then considered to be primitive musical cultures and represented the natural music for young children. Both sets of assumptions, that certain musical cultures were primitive and the close association of primitiveness with the naturalness of young children would be challenged today.

An Orff lesson is immediately recognisable by its distinctive pedagogy and by the sounds of Orff instruments. Playing barred instruments is often thought to be the signature activity that distinguishes Orff from other methods. Many stress that Orff is not intended to be a fixed method. Yet Orff-affiliated teachers recommend pedagogical strategies that are quite clearly defined and would seem, therefore, to constitute a method. For example, the Orff approach offers specific ways of structuring a lesson and the longer-term curriculum. Progression should move from simple to complex, from rhythm through to harmony and from pentatonic (five-note) to major (seven-note) modes. However, it is important to emphasise that the heart of the approach is the integration of rhythmic speech, rhyme, song and movement and combinations of these different media in improvising.

The Orff approach aims to build on what children bring to the session. Teachers should take their ideas and contributions, scaffolding their musical experiences and lead them to explore and discover musical concepts for themselves. In this way there are similarities with other child-centred and constructivist approaches. At the same time, because the Orff method offers ways in which children can be simultaneously engaged in group activities playing different parts, it includes successful strategies for working with larger numbers of children. There is a collaborative and social dimension to the nature of learning that heralds later theoretical conceptions of sociocultural learning (see p. 107).

Some are critical of the Orff approach for its assumptions about children's musical play and improvisation – that it begins with simple, parred down, repetitive structures and that children need to be given limited musical materials to channel their improvisation. The route into musical creativity which is explained and illustrated in Orff materials is via structured improvisation that reduces the possibilities and options. Children's creative musical play, critics would argue, when left to their own devices is more complex and imaginative than these reduced musical materials will allow. Others criticise the pedagogy for spending too long on these limited materials and musical styles. However, it is often pointed out that Orff's intention was for an imaginative, improvisatory approach and that some contemporary versions of the approach may have lost touch with this intention.

The present-day influence of the Orff Schulwerk on early childhood music education is mainly indirect. While some teachers may have attended training courses, accessed source materials and adopted the method keeping closely to its principles, this is rare. The use of movement, including body percussion, as a pedagogical medium to reinforce musical learning has become a standard teaching technique. The barred Orff-type instruments have now become a familiar part of educational resources. The playing of drones, ostinati, pentatonic patterns and block chords to songs is a familiar practice derived from the Orff approach. This practice connects well with the Kodály method particularly since both approaches suggest that the use of the pentatonic (five-note) scale is appropriate in the first stages of music learning. The pedagogical strategy of extracting one musical motif or phrase to be played on instruments so that children can accompany songs or recordings and thus 'get inside' the music, has translated successfully into more recent approaches that seek to incorporate music from a diversity of musical styles and cultures. However in early childhood general practice Orff instruments are more typically set out for children to use in free play and free choice improvisation activities, rather than structured and guided improvisation. The presence of educational percussion instruments has freed up possibilities for music education practices and the Orff approach – directly or indirectly – has certainly broadened the scope of music education pedagogy.

Bibliography

Carley, J. M. (1977). The central role of music in education. In I. M. Carley (ed.), *Orff Re-Echoes: Selections from the Orff Echo and the supplements*, pp. 79–81. Chagrin Falls, OH: American Orff-Schulwerk Association.

Orff, C. (1973). *Orff-Schulwerk: Past and future*. Orff Institute Yearbook. Reprinted as Orff Echo Supplement. Cleveland, OH: American Orff-Schulwerk Association.

Orff, C. and Keetman, G. (1976). *Music for Children*, vols. 1–5 (trans. M. Murray). London: Schott and Co. (Original work in German published 1950–1954).

9 Zoltán Kodály: Singing to Develop Musicianship

> We can produce better musicians only if we can bring about a thorough reorganisation in our methods of teaching music ... There must be a strenuous attempt to replace music that comes from the fingers and the mechanical playing of instruments with music from the soul and based on singing.
>
> (Kodály, 1965, p. 2)

In Hungary, from the 1940s onwards, the composer Zoltán Kodály initiated a music education method from a foundation of Hungarian folk music. In the Kodály method, or Kodály concept as it is also termed, singing and solfa training are the primary means for developing musicianship.

Although he is sometimes described as the creator of the Kodály method, this is not strictly correct as Kodály did not devise a comprehensive method. Instead, he laid down a set of principles for a music education that he hoped all children would receive and he wrote some first materials. Kodály's principles have been elaborated in practice by the many educators who followed in his footsteps. From the 1960s onwards the Kodály method travelled to other countries and continues to be very influential on early childhood music education practice world-wide.

Zoltán Kodály (1882–1967)

Zoltán Kodály was a composer and ethnomusicologist who was very interested in music education. As a music student in Budapest Kodály had become interested in folk music and he, with others, collected folk songs of Hungary and nearby regions over many years. These folk songs influenced his compositional style and with Béla Bartók he created a new style of art music based on folk music. After a history of foreign domination, Hungary was beginning to become conscious of its national identity and to value its own culture.

In the 1940s, Kodály turned his attention to music education and wrote an essay about music in the kindergarten in which he suggested that music is a 'subconscious keystone of Hungarian-ness' (Kodály, 1974). He considered it was important for children to know their musical heritage.

DOI: 10.4324/9781003331193-13

Throughout the 1940s and 1950s Kodály worked to improve music education in Hungary. With a colleague, he taught daily music lessons in Kecskemét using his own materials as a teaching experiment. This experiment was so successful that it led to the establishment of music primary schools across Hungary.

Philosophy

The philosophy guiding Kodály's educational work is that music makes an important contribution to the holistic development – intellectual, emotional, physical, social and spiritual – of every child. Kodály believed strongly that music belongs to everyone and every child is innately musical. Therefore all children have a right to an education in music that begins as early as possible. His aim was to instil a love of music in children based on musical knowledge and understanding rooted in first hand, active music-making experiences. These experiences should focus on aural work and vocal skills as the foundation from which a genuine musicianship based on aural ability will grow. Children's music education, Kodály believed, should draw on the traditional music of childhood: lullabies, childhood chants and rhymes, folk songs and singing games.

Kodály aimed to raise the general level of musical 'taste' in Hungarian society. He stressed that the musical materials used with young children must be of the best artistic quality. This placed a responsibility on teachers to introduce children to folk music and Western art music at its best.

Key Text

Lois Choksy. (1974). *The Kodály Method: Comprehensive music education from infant to adult*. Englewood Cliffs, NJ: Prentice-Hall.

Principles

For children to sing and to listen attentively lie at the heart of the Kodály method. Children are given plenty of opportunities to sing, almost always unaccompanied, and to take part in singing games and playful activities with a music-learning purpose. The method is sequential moving from direct, embodied experience of sound and rhythms to visual representations and finally abstract concepts. Teachers first aim to develop an internalised sense of pulse, pitch and rhythm that is intuitive – or unconscious as Kodály educators would say – and then, through a range of pedagogical strategies, to bring that intuitive understanding to a conscious level. The 'making conscious' process involves first the translation of direct experience into other modes such as spoken and sung syllables and visual symbols. The final stage is to present children with simplified notations and later full notations and ask them to recognise and read the written version. Here is the pedagogical sequence of activity.

- Build intuitive understanding through embodied experience.
- Make that understanding conscious.
- Practise it.
- Use and apply it in reading and improvising activities.

The method recommends that the content of music is broken down into small steps that build from the simple to the complex. It aims to move from what the children know musically and can do now, extending step-by-step to what they do not know. These steps are considered to map onto children's musical development. So, for example, the singing starts with simple two or three note chants within young children's comfortable singing range and then gradually expands the pitch range.

The teacher will ask questions that invite the children to problem-solve or analyse in order to develop their musical thinking and understanding. They will ask questions such as, how does this rhythm compare to this one? Do you hear a new note in this phrase? Is this higher, lower, faster, slower?

The musical objectives are to:

- Sing, play, and move from memory, a large number of traditional folksongs belonging to the children's musical heritage. The repertoire includes children's traditional rhymes, chants and songs such as counting rhymes, the songs that accompany circle games and skipping rhymes, folk songs of their own culture and other cultures.
- Achieve mastery of musical skills, such as musical reading and writing, singing and part-singing. The lessons will include practice exercises and music examples for sight reading and other learning activities.
- Improvise and compose, using their known musical vocabulary at each developmental stage.
- Perform (usually in singing), listen to, and analyse music, usually from the European classical tradition.

There is a focus on the development of musical skills in the Kodály approach. The skills being developed are:

- singing and vocal development
- aural skills
- rhythmic movement and coordination
- musical memory and inner hearing
- knowledge of notation symbols and being able to read and write them, and
- improvisation skills.

Older children will make simple compositions using the musical materials they have acquired and they may incorporate instruments thus learning how to handle and play instruments, usually educational percussion.

Early Start

Kodály advocated for music education to begin as early in a child's life as possible, so the method has evolved to be especially suitable for young children.

Mother-Tongue

The term 'mother-tongue' songs refers to the traditional songs of a child's heritage. According to Kodály principles, mother-tongue songs should be the first songs introduced to children. However, the changing demographic of school populations in the twenty-first century compared to 1940s Hungary, means that it is no longer appropriate to select repertoire to reinforce one cultural heritage. Many reinterpret the idea of mother tongue in more general terms to mean that the repertoire should be drawn from an eclectic collection of children's songs and singing games.

The Voice

Musicianship and musical literacy are developed through the voice, as the child's first instrument. Care is taken to match singing and singing activities to the children's developing vocal capabilities by selecting songs that have the correct pitch range and level of melodic complexity. Songs which have simple, clear and repetitive melodic lines are easier for learning singers to sing successfully, and so these form a core repertoire.

Falling Minor-Third and Pentatonic

Kodály – as did Orff – considered the pentatonic (five-note) scale to the most suitable for young children. Hungarian folk music is largely pentatonic. So first songs use a limited pitch range and typically focus on the minor third, the 'so-mi' interval. This interval creates the chant which is often sung by young children in their spontaneous singing play. To this interval the 'la' or 'do' is added so that the tones of the pentatonic scale are gradually built up.

The teacher will make sure that songs are sung at the correct pitch for children's developing vocal abilities by using a tuning fork or some other means of providing the starting pitch, for example, a set of chime bars or a phone app. Opinion varies as to the best pitch range for children's singing, but in general adults tend to sing in a lower pitch range than children. Being asked to sing in a pitch range that does not match their vocal ability can take away the child's ability to sing a song accurately – or even to connect with singing the song at all and become frustrated. Therefore Kodály educators place great importance on the correct pitching of songs for children's developing vocal range.

Inner Hearing

The aim is to train aural ability, often referred to as inner hearing, through unaccompanied singing. Adding any form of instrumental accompaniment or backing track is discouraged. Teachers typically incorporate singing activities that allow children to sing solo so that each child can hear their own singing clearly and the teachers can monitor the progress of children's singing ability. Kodály proposed that two-part singing should be introduced at an early stage because it also helps children to become secure with pitching their voices accurately. Simple rounds or songs with an ostinato provide inroads into part singing that are typically included in Kodály repertoire.

Movement and Musical Games

Kodály was influenced by Dalcroze eurhythmics. Musical games involve children in stepping, tapping and clapping, mainly to the beat or simple rhythm patterns. It is considered important to establish children's ability to maintain a steady beat or to find the beat in a song.

Tonic Solfa

Solfa is the set of syllables, do, re, mi, fa, so, la, ti, which are sung to each tone of the major scale. These syllables are considered to be more singable and memorable than other ways of naming pitches with letters or numbers. Singing with solfa helps to promote aural memory for intervals and in this way the sense of tonality – how the different pitches relate to one another – is developed.

Kodály was not the first to use solfa, it had been developed by others before him, but he incorporated it as a central element of the method. He wrote a graded sequence of teaching materials to develop sight-singing and aural ability based on Hungarian folk music.

The Kodály approach uses a moveable do system in which the 'do' is always the first degree of the major scale, hence its name, tonic solfa. This preserves the position of the semitones between the 3–4 (mi–fa) and 7–8 (ti–do) degrees of the major tonality. In many European music systems, the 'do' is always middle C, as in the solfège system that is part of the Dalcroze method. There are pros and cons with each system.

Hand Signs

Each solfa syllable is represented by a hand sign. (Illustrations of the hand signs can be quickly found online). Kodály adopted the hand signs from earlier music educators and choir leaders.

Using the hand signs provides children with both a visual and a physical representation of the pitches, their direction and melodic shape. The hand shapes help to reinforce the feel of each pitch within the scale. The dominant tones of the major triad – do, mi, so – are shown with clear, quite strong hand shapes, whereas the intermediary tones have hand-signs that lead to or from the more dominant tones.

The hand signs are a useful teaching tool, enabling the teacher to create opportunities for all children to participate in aural activities, often framed as games, involving pitch recognition. Using the hand signs also offers an intermediary step in learning to sight-sing before learning to read from written staff notation.

Rhythm Syllables

Rhythm syllables are a set of verbal syllables that are used as a learning tool for reading and writing rhythms. There are a number of variations of rhythm syllables and the Kodály system is slightly different to other systems, such as, for example, the French time names, a system which is also well known. The small variations in syllables between different systems are less important than ensuring that the syllables easy to pronounce and comfortable to use within the children's first language, and that they are used consistently.

Educators also select words with syllables that match rhythm patterns. Teachers often take the rhythm of words or short phrases from songs in the children's repertoire. The use of word rhythms allow for practice and recognition activities.

The main advantages for any system of rhythm syllables is that children quickly learn to use them. A disadvantage of using syllables for rhythm patterns is that they connect with the metre less well. They can also tend to be a little wooden and work best with simpler rhythms, rather than rhythms that have interesting variety and 'groove'.

'Stick' or Solfa Notation

This is a combination of rhythmic stick symbols and solfa which is used as a preliminary stage in learning to read standard staff notation. It supports children in the first stages of linking what they hear with visual symbols. It enables children to read and also to write music using a relative, rather than a fixed system of notation on a staff and it helps children to develop an understanding of intervals and tonal and rhythmic patterns.

Image of Childhood

Kodály's view of the child is of one who needs to be socialised into national musical culture, strongly guided by the structured curriculum. The emphasis is on the child as a blank sheet, to be trained musically by adults. There is less focus on the child as having independent agency or allowing them to explore their own musical interests and backgrounds.

The Method in Practice

A group of eight 4-year-olds sit in a circle on small chairs with their teacher. She sings a short opening phrase, greeting each child in turn, on two notes only, a falling minor third (so–mi). Each child, individually, sings their name and a greeting in a responding phrase. The singing is unaccompanied, and before she starts to sing, the teacher has pinged a tuning fork close to her ear to check she is starting on a pitch that sits within the children's comfortable vocal range. Partway through the activity, the teacher changes the pitch of her opening phrase to see if the children will hear the change and respond at the new pitch. They do, and she comments – 'did you hear me change my voice? I sang a bit lower.' She changes the pitch of the song more times and asks the children to notice and tune into the changes.

She then goes on to sing the short phrase with solfa – 'so-mi' and adds hand signs to the solfa. The children automatically join in with singing solfa syllables and showing the hand signs. They have been introduced to these already and know how to use them. The teacher claps two rhythm patterns from the song and adds rhythm syllables. The children copy her clapping and chant the rhythm syllables.

The teacher:

- begins with a short song that is pitched within the children's vocal range
- provides for each child to learn to sing it through individual imitation
- develops the children's aural discrimination by changing the starting pitch of the song
- translates the song into solfa syllables and rhythm syllables
- translates the solfa and rhythm syllables into visual symbols such as hand signs or stick notation
- introduces verbal terms (e.g. lower pitch), and
- encourages the children to compare and name.

This short, typical opening activity will then be followed by more songs, many of which will have simple movements or games incorporated into them in the style of children's traditional singing games. Typically the educator models the song first for children to imitate in unison and then offers the children opportunities to sing individually. Singing solo enables children to hear their own voices clearly and to listen attentively to the sound they are producing. This helps them to learn to control their voices and sing in tune. With a class of children, it is usually only practical for children to sing solo in short call and response songs, or single phrases of a song.

Many teachers developed the methods and materials of Hungarian preschool music education under the guidance of Kodály from 1947 until his death in 1967 and they continued the work thereafter. They have produced detailed pedagogical guidance and attractive song material, widely disseminated through publications and accompanying workshops. The published materials that accompany the Kodály method are detailed in their instructions to the educator, reflecting what is primarily an adult-centric and structured approach.

Katalin Forrai and Jean Sinor

Notable among these disciple teachers was Katalin Forrai (1926–2004). She was a teacher, teacher trainer and researcher and taught music to toddlers in Budapest for over 50 years. Her book, *Music in Preschool* (first published in Hungarian in 1974) was translated and adapted by Jean Sinor (in 1988) to suit the education of pre-school children in the USA. Forrai's early childhood music education philosophy emphasised the importance of developmentally appropriate curriculum design, the use of quality folk songs as well as singing games from the children's mother-tongue culture and the importance of nurturing the child's emotions, imagination and creativity through playful activity. In the translated version Jean Sinor explains how Hungarian folksong has musical differences to Anglo-American folksong and how, therefore, the repertoire in the translated book was adapted. Katalin Forrai insisted that each nation should discover its own musical heritage to teach the youngest children. The book remains a detailed and informative exposition of how to apply the approach to practice.

Key Text

Katalin Forrai. (1988). *Music in Preschool*, translated and adapted by Jean Sinor. Budapest: Corvina.

Comments and Connections

Reading many accounts of the dissemination of the Kodály method and from my own experiences, Kodály and his followers insisted on certain pedagogical tenets with an authority and conviction that tend to characterise the method. While there is no doubt that these tenets help to maintain pedagogical standards and disseminate certain effective tools and techniques of practice, they can also reinforce a belief that there is one correct way that must be adhered to.

It is also useful to remember that the Hungarian system of generously funded public pre-schools provided the context for Kodály-based pre-school experiences to be nationally organised, supported and to flourish. In many countries such pre-school systems and national support do not exist.

During the 1960s and thereafter Kodály educators found an obvious link between their pedagogical principles and the emerging ideas of children's musical development, specifically in connecting with models of singing development. Ensuring that first songs match young children's singing capabilities so that they can learn to sing with accuracy is a major contribution of the Kodály method to early childhood music education. The key phrase, 'developmentally appropriate practice' became central to Kodály pedagogy. In addition the pedagogical strategies of concept development and sequencing of learning in progressive steps have been strengthened by links with Piaget's and Bruner's theories of children's conceptual learning (Houlahan and Tacka, 2008).

However there is criticism. One criticism is that if adhered to strictly the method can become a narrow course of musical training, adult-centred, didactic and somewhat inflexible. The principle of limiting the pitch and rhythms of early songs can result in the musical content being less varied, some even say dull and repetitive. Recent research studies into young children's singing abilities (Gudmundsdottir, 2020) have demonstrated that young children are often more capable as singers than the models of singing development may have suggested. This implies that children could be offered more demanding and musically varied singing repertoire at younger ages than the Kodály method usually recommends. Some point to the songs that today's children hear as part of their everyday media experiences and which introduce them to much more melodic variety than the limited pitch and rhythm songs of Kodály repertoire. Moreover children are hearing and absorbing a wide variety of musical styles in their everyday listening experiences, beyond the traditional folk song repertoire.

The method with its focus on solfa and rhythm learning leads towards music literacy; more so than other pedagogical approaches. While this focus develops children's aural and musical skills, some say, the focus is too formal, too early. They suggest that children should have greater freedom to explore and discover music in child-centred approaches. To counterbalance this tendency for over-formality, many of today's music educators prefer to refer to the Kodály method, not as a method but as Kodály-inspired music education. This shift in terminology reflects the fact that the method, they claim, is adaptable and evolving – although how flexible it is in reality might be open to question.

Kodály was concerned with what he saw as the erosion of Hungarian national culture by outside influences and he saw education as the most effective means to counteract those influences. He believed that young children should be taught music using only their local folk music in order to avoid 'cultural confusion'. In wider social and cultural terms, the goal of advancing an education based on nationalistic principles would be carefully considered by educators. As the approach has spread worldwide, questions are raised as to how an approach so rooted in Hungarian folk music and European art music can meet the educational needs of present-day children in many different countries. In musical terms alone, as Forrai and Sinor explained very clearly in their book, the melodic patterns underlying the Kodály method are in keeping with the tonalities and melodic patterning of Hungarian folk melodies and not those of other cultures. The principle of starting with songs that represent the children's own culture suggests that every country should source and select its own materials and adapt the method. Yet given the increasing diversity of children in today's classrooms, finding repertoire to connect with the cultural heritage of all the children becomes an almost impossible aim. In short, there are no easy answers. But songs are not neutral, they carry historical, cultural and social resonances and the selection of repertoire in respect of the children sitting before us needs careful thought.

The Three Methods Side by Side

Placing the three methods, Dalcroze, Orff and Kodály, side-by-side draws attention to some important similarities and some key differences that are useful to set out in clear terms. The conviction that music education should develop the innate musicality of *all* children and aim for musical experience to precede formal knowledge underpins the philosophies of all three. But they aimed to fulfil these purposes in different ways.

- Kodály gave central importance to the voice and to sight-singing. Singing makes an important contribution to both Orff and Dalcroze (a fact often overlooked with respect to Dalcroze) but is less prominent and integrated into the other forms of activity.
- Orff incorporated musical instruments designed for educational purpose, whereas Kodály and Dalcroze did not. Dalcroze teachers use hand-held percussion, traditionally small hand drums.
- Dalcroze includes whole body movements and rhythmic movement exercises, whereas in both Kodály and Orff, movement is secondary and combined with rhymes and song, often as body percussion.
- Kodály is the most structured and didactic method. Orff and Dalcroze are less structured.
- Musical creativity and improvisation are foundational to Orff, also an important element in Dalcroze but less so in Kodály. Kodály aims to increase musical abilities which may then be applied in creative musical experiences as a final stage.
- Musical literacy is a key aim of Kodály, but less so with Orff and Dalcroze.

Short training courses which introduce the individual methods are widespread. However attention in these courses is typically focussed on content, teaching tips and activity ideas. Seldom is their time – or sometimes the inclination – for in-depth discussion of the origins, philosophy or principles of the method. As a result, methods often become an end in themselves and teaching the method takes priority over identifying the learning needs of the children and selecting pedagogical strategies that will best serve those needs.

All the methods call up the past, turning traditions of both folk music and art music into education processes that have become defined and reified. Traditional learning is assumed to be necessary both for children's own future and the future of a society. Some would argue that the core philosophies continue to be highly relevant and that the ways they are implemented in practice are always evolving to keep in step with the times. They also claim that pedagogical strategies such as learning through movement and playful singing activities are developmentally appropriate for young children and should be fundamental to any music education approach. Others would argue that the methods, including the pedagogical principles, are so steeped in European musical cultures and social histories, that they cannot shake off their origins. Meeting the challenges of designing pedagogies for today's society and children requires a more radical response and a rethink of the very fundamentals of how we teach as well as what we teach.

Bibliography

Gudmundsdottir, H. R. (2020). Revisiting singing proficiency in three-year-olds. *Psychology of Music*, 48(2), 283–296.

Houlahan, M. and Tacka, P. (2008). *Kodály Today: A Cognitive Approach to Elementary Music Education*. Oxford: Oxford University Press.

Kodály, Z. (1974). Music in the kindergarten. In F. Bónis (Ed.), *Selected writings of Zoltán Kodály* (trans. L. Halápy and F. Macnicol), pp. 127–148. Budapest: Corvina Press. (Original work published 1941).

Kodály, Z. (1965). *Fifty Five Two-Part Exercises*. London: Boosey and Hawkes. (Original work published 1954.)

Part IV

In looking at the history of learning theories and their influence on music education a key shift from the 1960s onwards was the growth in the psychological study of children. Part IV introduces the work of three psychologists, Piaget, Vygotsky and Bruner, who have each had a profound influence on how we understand the processes of learning and teaching. In each section I first explain the theory of each psychologist and then go on to introduce music educators who adapted those theories to their music teaching for young children.

Until the 1970s the psychology of music focused mainly on aural perception. Researchers measured children's ability to perceive the elements of music such as pitch, rhythm, melody and harmony in straightforward experimental tests. Beginning in the 1960s the focus shifted away from these simple perception studies. Piaget's theories prompted research into children's musical cognition and musical development. Researchers started to ask, how do young children understand music? What are the sources of this understanding? What might be innate and what might be learned from experience? How does their musical understanding develop?

Bruner's interest in the processes of learning and teaching inspired music educators who applied them in designing curriculum and pedagogical materials for early childhood music education. The writings of these educators provide detailed explanations for conceptual learning in music and how to promote that learning.

Vygotsky's sociocultural theories of learning gave impetus to a new wave of activity in music education research that sought to understand young children's music learning within social and cultural contexts. Based on those new understandings, educators went on to propose revised approaches to music learning and teaching as a social process.

DOI: 10.4324/9781003331193-14

10 Jean Piaget: Children's Ways of Understanding

> The goal of education is not to increase the amount of knowledge but to create the possibilities for a child to invent and discover.
>
> (Piaget, 1952, p. 412)

Piaget's theories were both cognitive and developmental in that he sought to explain how (1) children process information, how children learn in other words, and (2) how that processing changes – how it develops – as children grow older. His theories dominated developmental psychology in the 1960s and 1970s. The aim of this type of research by Piaget, and by others carrying out similar research, was to develop general, concise theories that were thought to be universal, that is, the same for all children.

Piaget did not explicitly relate his theory to education. However, because he offered so many ideas about cognitive development, his work has been highly influential on educational practice, including music education. His work introduced the key idea that, in order to learn most effectively, children need to progress along their natural pathway of cognitive development. This brought about an important shift in educational thinking. Teachers were no longer mere transmitters of knowledge to children who were mere absorbers of knowledge. The implications of Piaget's theorising were that teachers should think more carefully about what and how they teach in relation to the developing cognitive abilities of children.

The influence of his theories filtered into music education in the mid-1970s and early 1980s. They inspired research that looked at how children process musical information and searched for models of musical development which would be common to all children.

Jean Piaget (1896–1980)

Born in Neuchâtel, Switzerland, Piaget lived for most of his life in Geneva. He originally studied zoology and received his doctorate from the University of Neuchâtel in 1918. He then spent two years at the Sorbonne involved in research that evaluated children's responses to an intelligence test. In applying these tests Piaget realised that children of the same age were prone to making the same errors and he began to wonder whether younger children possessed different cognitive processes to older children and adults. He returned to Switzerland and worked first at the University of Neuchâtel and later Geneva University, where he remained for the rest of his life. He married Valentine Chátenay in 1923 and their observations of their three children served as a basis for many of his later theories.

Theory

The idea of dividing a child's cognitive development into a series of stages was a key theme in most of Piaget's early work in the 1920s. His detailed observations, initially of his own children, and careful experiments allowed him to identify sequential stages in various aspects of child development. There were two major influences from Piaget's work. One, his work suggested that children's development, as individuals, was fixed by a set of sequential stages. The stages shifted in type from stage to stage. Two, it emphasised a gulf between the abilities of children and of adults. Children approached and understood the world in significantly different ways to adults that were more than simply lack of experience.

Piaget rejected the behaviourists' idea that learning is a passive process and children merely absorb fixed and pre-given knowledge. For Piaget, any change in behaviour comes about through thinking and processing information, not simply through rote learning and imitation. Instead, he proposed that learners actively construct knowledge by creating and testing their own theories of the world. His theory is thus constructivist because he thought that children have to construct their own thought processes. These thought processes arise from children's interactions with their environment and their attempts to make sense of those interactions. Piaget focussed on children's play with their material environment rather than, for example as Vygotsky emphasised, their interactions with other people in a social environment.

Piaget proposed that children's thinking, their cognition, progresses in stages as a result both of biological maturing and their real-world experience. For Piaget children act on objects in their environment and internalise the results of those actions. In this way they evolve ways of thinking about those objects. He referred to these thought-actions as operations. Thinking is thus a form of internalised action. Music educators, for example, may provide very young children with small percussion instruments that make an interesting sound and children explore them, hearing the sounds they make, and their perceptions of sound bond with their actions.

As they process more and more direct, real-world experiences, children's thinking becomes more abstract and more detached from action. So while young children may need physical and concrete experiences from which to learn, older children may be able to work with more abstract representations such as verbal descriptions and symbolic notations. Piaget theorised these changes from concrete to abstract as distinct stages of cognitive development.

Stages of Cognitive Development

Piaget's stage model of child development is well known (Piaget, 1952). For Piaget, all children pass through the same four stages of cognitive development in exactly the same order.

1. 0–2 years, sensorimotor learning: learning through motor activity and manipulation of objects, and through their senses.
2. 2–7 years, pre-operational learning: the transformation of sensorimotor to symbolic learning. Children typically use language, nonverbal gestures and imagery to organise information about the world. This stage still remains rooted in the material environment; it is not yet abstract.
3. 7–11 years, concrete operations: an increasing ability to classify objects and events using abstract symbols but children commonly still require concrete examples to anchor their ideas.
4. 11 onwards: formal operations, thought processes typical of an adult.

Nowadays most do not believe that these stages exist in the way that Piaget originally described them for two main reasons. First, Piaget saw each stage as containing quite clearly defined sets of activities following certain logical rules, but many subsequent researchers found that these activities are much less precise than Piaget had suggested. Second, the theory does not take into account the context of children's lives and therefore does not recognise sufficiently the influence of social and cultural diversity.

Schemas

Schemas (sometimes referred to as mental models, scripts, or frames) are structures that organise knowledge in the mind. They are the 'building blocks' of knowledge that enable children to form a mental representation of the world. The formation of schemas is thought to help children to connect new information with pre-existing knowledge, skills and concepts and thereby expand their existing schemas.

Teaching approaches that allow for discovery, problem-solving, comparing, organising and elaborating experiences and ideas help children to form schemas, such as:

- Activities that focus children's experiences on certain concepts. *A 2-year-old plays with a guitar laid flat on the floor. He first strums the strings with one hand, but then discovers how to pluck a single string with one finger, listening carefully to the sound and its resonance. He repeats this activity many, many times, consolidating his perception and association of action and sound.*
- Problem-based learning. The educator sets up a situation whereby children try to apply existing knowledge or skills to a task that has a higher level of challenge. *The nursery practitioner finds other stringed instruments, a*

small zither and a ukulele. *The 2-year-old now applies his plucking action to new instruments and discovers new sounds.*
- Comparisons and analogies. These add depth or can address misconceptions. *Now the practitioner introduces an mbira (one designed for educational use). The 2-year-old tries the same plucking action but finds it makes a small, dull sound. He soon discovers a slightly different plucking action with one finger, on the end of the metal keys, that will make a more resonant, ringing sound. His original action-plus-perception schema needed to change when faced with this new challenge.*
- Elaborating concepts with more examples in different musical situations, to strengthen concepts and transfer them. Older children with language skills can be asked to describe in words. *The practitioner collects together the stringed instruments and includes the mbira for a circle time with 4-year-olds in the nursery. With these children she can move more quickly through the manipulation and discovery steps, starting then to describe and explain the differences in playing technique, sound, pitch and timbre.*

Thus, for Piaget, to explore, change and transform objects is how children learn and these operations, as he termed them, are the essence of the child's knowledge. Learning through activity and children coming to understand music through their own efforts is key. Their activities and achievements should be evaluated in accordance with the child's developing understanding, rather than in comparison with any external or imposed forms of knowledge. In other words, the educator does not intervene to correct or direct the child but tries to work out what they are thinking on their own terms and then decides how to extend that thinking.

Teaching as Facilitation

Piaget proposed that learning through discovery and problem-solving skills are required for new learning to occur and so this implies that educators need to consider what concepts children are meeting in their musical experiences, how concepts link together and in particular how new concepts will build on children's prior knowledge. Therefore, learning should be child-centred and the teacher needs to be a facilitator within the classroom. Planning should aim to provide children with opportunities to discover and construct their musical understanding. The focus is therefore on the process of learning, rather than on an end product or arriving at a performance.

Adaptation Processes

Piaget later expanded his theory to explain how children adjust their thinking, their schemas, when faced with new experiences that present them with new information. They may *assimilate* the new information, meaning that they make sense of the new experience in terms of their existing schemas. Or they may make small adjustments, that is, they *accommodate* them to fit their existing knowledge, thereby creating an *equilibrium* (balance). If a new experience cannot be assimilated or accommodated, it causes *disequilibrium* which then prompts a major changes in the child's thinking perhaps shifting them to another level of thinking.

Image of Childhood

Piaget viewed cognitive development as essentially a biological process that follows the same pathway for all children. It can lead to a tendency to measure and assess children against milestones that are thought to be the same for all children and to take less account of their individuality and the contexts of their lives.

It is often said that in Piaget's eyes children act like little scientists in that they experiment with things in order to try to understand their world. His image of childhood focuses on cognition and logical thinking rather than emotions and imaginative thinking.

Key Text

Jean Piaget and Bärbel Inhelder. (1969). *The Psychology of the Child*. Washington, DC: Prentice-Hall.

Influences on Music Education

In the 1960s and 1970s Piaget's theories inspired research into children's musical cognition and musical development. Several researchers started to look for age related characteristics of children's musical responses and abilities. The underlying assumption in these Piagetian studies of children's musical understanding was that there are stages in children's development when they are able to grasp certain aspects of musical knowledge and perform certain musical tasks. There was a strong conviction that better understanding of children's musical abilities and stages of development would be very informative to educators.

The music psychologist David Hargreaves published a landmark book in 1986 that reviewed the field of developmental psychology of music up to that date and aimed to explain the role it could play in music education. He stated that insights into children's musical development ought to have a great deal to say about how children should be taught.

Key Text

David Hargreaves. (1986). *The Developmental Psychology of Music*. Cambridge: Cambridge University Press.

Sensorimotor Explorations

Over the course of three years from 2002 to 2005, François Delalande, collaborating with early childhood colleagues in Northern Italy, carefully observed individual children aged 10 to 40 months when they were playing with instruments on their own (Delalande, 2015). The children attended daycare centres. The research team noticed how the children found actions to explore the possibilities of the instruments and interpreted the children's sensorimotor explorations according to Piagetian theory. The team suggested that when the children's actions produced the sounds children expected to hear they accommodated them to their existing schema, but when the sounds were unexpected they caused disequilibrium. They noticed that the children would repeat the actions producing the unexpected sounds many times as the children attempted to make sense of them and alter their schema to accommodate them. This research project demonstrates how a contemporary application of Piagetian theory can continue to be informative, particularly the application of ideas drawn from schema theory and sensorimotor thinking.

Pre-operational to Concrete Operations: Conservation

According to Piaget conservation is a characteristic of the shift to more logical thinking that takes place around 7 to 8 years of age. Conservation is the understanding that something stays the same in quantity even though its appearance changes. For example, younger children might believe that lengthening a row of counters (by spreading them out) increases the number or that squashing a ball of plasticine flat reduces its volume.

Some of the first attempts to apply Piagetian concepts to music cognition focussed on the idea of conservation. In the early 1960s Marilyn Pflederer at the University of Illinois applied the idea of conservation to children's musical thinking with respect to melody, rhythm and metre (Pflederer, 1964). Children were played a short melody followed by a version of it in which one property such as pitch level, tempo or rhythmic duration was transformed while everything else about the melody remained the same. Children were then asked whether the two versions were 'the same' or 'different'. In one of her first studies she asked children whether a melody remained the same, regardless of changes in tempo. Approximately half of the 5-year-old children identified the melody as being the same, with this rising to over 90 per cent by 8 years of age. Pre-operational children, it was proposed, cannot conserve and would either say the melodies were the same *or* that they were different, but not both. Concrete operational children should be able to conserve, that is, they recognise the sameness and the difference. The results of her studies suggested that children would improve on this kind of musical conservation task with age.

Just as many have pointed out weaknesses in Piaget's original experiments of conservation, so too there are problems when the same kinds of experiments are transferred to music. For example, young children have to rely on their musical memories when they are asked if a melody is the same at two very different speeds. Five-year-olds may be less able to remember the melody. Add to this the problem that younger children may also not understand the test instructions accurately and already two possible flaws with Pflederer's research method are brought to light.

While we might now be sceptical about the findings from these conservation studies – and from other research which similarly attempted to apply Piagetian theory – they are valuable examples of how researchers and educators have attempted to apply psychological theories in order to better understand the detail of children's musical thinking.

Models of Musical Development

There have been many attempts to arrive at models of musical development, either for musical ability in general, or for specific modes of activity such as singing, moving, aural ability and improvising. There are many such models and it is beyond the scope of this book to explain them all. Besides, the focus of this book is applications of theory to practice.

The usefulness of models of development to teachers' practice helps to explain why developmental theory became such a strong influence. The idea of stages of development that are the same for all children allows educators to make general decisions about the abilities and learning style of a group of children, all of the same age. Developmental theory holds that while there may be some individual variation, children's abilities, and certainly the way they best learn, would cluster around a common set of expectations. For instance, having in mind a model of singing development allows teachers to select songs and vocal activities which take into account what children are able to do, as singers, at certain ages and stages. Thus the concept of developmentally appropriate practice, or DAP as it is often known, arose.

The Theory in Practice

Marjorie Glynne-Jones wrote a guide to music education in English primary schools, published in 1974, that applied Piagetian theory to practice and was informed by a clearly stated theory of child-centred and, as she termed it, 'developmental education'. The book begins with a chapter on early development stating firmly that all educators need to understand musical development from birth. The follow-on chapters provide numerous examples of young children exploring music and musical ideas in educational settings. These are described in words and through notations, some transcribed by Glynne-Jones and some represented by children's own drawn notations. The descriptions are accompanied by transcripts of the children's talk with their teacher.

In these ways the book illustrates a constructivist classroom, in which the focus shifts from the teacher to the children. What the children do, draw and say is central because these sources of information all provide clues as to the children's musical thinking. The classroom is not a place where the teacher as expert pours knowledge into passive students; the children are assumed to be actively constructing their musical knowledge.

> A group of five year old boys decided to make a band. They marched round the classroom playing drums and cymbals rhythmically.
>
> The activity of this band of five year olds is characteristic of children's functioning when ideas are intuitively used. There is no mental analysis of the ideas for the view is a global one. During this pre-operational stage of intellectual development, children need to explore and experiment with as wide a selection of musical materials as possible, in order to build the foundations of ideas which later will become concrete, specific and capable of analysis.
>
> (Glynne-Jones, 1974, p. 13)

Her book illustrates a Piaget-based approach.

- Children are offered the freedom to play, learn through discovery and experiment with the materials of music in order to develop musical thinking. For this purpose the children have free access to resources (e.g. the drums and cymbals).
- Musical thinking is linked to children's internal (intuitive) representations of sensorimotor structures that will later become concrete.
- The teacher attempts to identify children's prior and current knowledge and to understand their musical thinking. This indicates what support or next steps the children need.
- The concepts of accommodation and assimilation require children to make their own discoveries and to explore different possibilities in open-ended activities. Prompting actions or verbal questions from the adult support this process at a later stage when the children's ideas are 'capable of analysis'.

Glynne-Jones writes, interestingly, that what children are observed by teachers to be doing by rote and imitation (a behaviourist approach), does not reveal their genuine musical understanding (Glynne-Jones, 1974, p. 135). Her book emphasises the need for educational process that builds musical understanding and concept development rather than the simple mechanistic, behavioural, learning of skills. She adopts the template of Piagetian staged theory by proposing that children's processes of musical learning are at first pre-operational and only become operational after the age of 7 years. She thus stresses the importance of children's concrete activity as necessary for their development of musical ideas and that thinking develops as their actions are internalised. It is only later, she writes, 'that they can learn at second-hand without being involved in the action themselves, or deal abstractly with the problem in hand without reference to the concrete' (ibid., p. 137).

Each chapter then focuses on a musical element – pitch, form, rhythm and so on – discussing how children gradually form musical concepts, again, by providing small scripts of teacher and child discussion that model the Piagetian inspired process of problem posing and questioning to develop children's understanding. As children explore and experiment, they draw conclusions, and, as exploration continues, they revisit those conclusions and may revise them.

Key Text

Marjorie Glynne-Jones. (1974). *Music.* Basingstoke: Macmillan.

Comments and Connections

Overall the influence of Piaget's ideas has been considerable. He transformed how educators understood children's learning and how, in turn, they understood their teaching role. His ideas inspired a huge amount of research in educational practice, including in music education. Some research directly applied his principles of children's cognition (e.g. schema theory, conservation), some was influenced by his general principles of discovery learning through play (e.g. sensorimotor exploration of instruments) and some was influenced by his staged theory of children's cognitive development.

A key legacy of Piaget's influence on the early years curriculum is child-centredness. Piaget had been preceded by philosopher-pedagogues who promoted a child-centred approach as far back as Froebel. But Piaget's theoretical work added a strong impetus to the development of pedagogies which put children at the centre and sought to reflect their needs and interests as the main drivers of their own learning. However this is freedom within certain limitations, prescribed by his ideas of competences defined by age and the limitations of freedom within whole class teaching. His theory perhaps also assumed that children should be naturally curious and there is a risk that children who do not appear to be motivated by exploratory activities were somehow not fitting a norm. We might wonder what happened to the 5-year-olds in Marjorie Glynn's classroom who did not want to join in the band or who perhaps found it too noisy?

Piaget's influence was also absorbed into the existing 'grand methods' of music education. When I studied Dalcroze eurhythmics at the Institut Jaques-Dalcroze, Geneva, in the early 1970s, Piaget was still professor at the University of Geneva. The tutors who taught Dalcroze pedagogy aligned Dalcroze principles with Piaget's theories of sensorimotor experience and schema. A conviction that young children learn music most effectively through sensorimotor experience is now well embedded in early childhood music education practice. The educators who continued Kodály's work absorbed developmental theory into the method and stressed the importance of marrying the sequence of the content with children's developing abilities

(Choksy, 1974). Certainly an important legacy for music education is Piaget's theoretical thinking around development and age-related changes. However this aspect is not without contention.

The major criticism surrounding Piaget's theories has centred on his theory of universal developmental stages: the assumption that all children develop in the same way. The two major reasons for these criticisms were mentioned earlier but are worth reiterating. (1) Universal stages do not take into account how children's social and cultural experiences shape their thinking. (2) The idea that children's thinking is always consistent within certain stages is not supported by the evidence as securely as Piaget initially believed. Later research has often revealed that children's abilities, needs and interests are much more varied than models imply and depend on a wide range of factors, not just biological maturation. Importantly too, children are often more capable than the original staged models have implied. The musical environment for young children has changed considerably. In just the last 10 or 20 years digital technologies have enabled children's lives to be filled with recorded sounds and music that emanate from all kinds of sources – toys, phones, televisions, car audio systems and more. If we assume babies and very young children are absorbing from their musical environments then it stands to reason that this generation of young children are acquiring more knowledge of music than in previous generations.

Developmental models become problematic in education when they are thought to be true and are adopted too literally. Following developmental models rigidly can result in concern to push children on and anxiety if they do not achieve predetermined milestones. Equally sticking to developmental models may result in having lower expectations children's capabilities and not enabling them to achieve more. They are useful, however, as templates for *how* children's learning might progress. They can inform planning and evaluations of children's learning, as a flexible set of guidelines.

With respect to models of development in music, one major problem is that they have been very sparsely informed by research with under-3-year-olds. There are obvious reasons for this shortage. Piagetian theory had suggested that the youngest children are not yet able to organise their thoughts in any meaningful way. This assumption had taken root and consequently there was not a strong incentive to study the very youngest children. It is only in more recent years that this age group has been given more attention and some assumptions about the musical abilities of the youngest children have been revised. Even then, in practical terms, babies and toddlers are difficult for researchers to access at home, or in daycare, whereas older children attend pre-school in larger numbers. And finally, special methods have to be devised in order to carry out research studies with babies and toddlers, often requiring equipment only available in university labs.

Piaget conceptualised cognitive development as a naturally evolving, biological process in lockstep with children's maturing. Piagetian theory tends, therefore, to encourage an approach to teaching which assumes that children cannot do things until a certain stage is reached and so holds back. Neither Vygotsky nor Bruner, as we will see, talked about age-related stages, preferring to see development as a continuous, unfolding process. Their theoretical perspectives encourage an approach which is more pro-active and assumes that learning can drive development and children can be supported to achieve more.

For Piaget language is seen as secondary to action, that is, thought precedes language. Vygotsky, in contrast, argued that language and thought go hand in hand. According to Piaget children need considerable direct, embodied and aural experience of music in order to form internal representations (schema) and only then will they be able to link representation with verbal terminology. For Vygotsky, naming, describing and talking about musical ideas will help children to form those ideas. This raises interesting challenges for music educators who should decide when and how to introduce verbal descriptions, names and terms in their teaching.

Bibliography

Choksy, L. (1974). *The Kodály Method: Comprehensive music education from infant to adult*. Englewood Cliffs, NJ: Prentice-Hall.

Delalande, F. (2015). *Naissance de la musique: Les explorations sonores de la première enfance*. Rennes: Presses Universitaires de Rennes.

Glynne-Jones, M. (1974). *Music*. Basingstoke: Macmillan.

Halpenny, A. M. and Pettersen, J. (2014). *Introducing Piaget: A guide for practitioners and students in early years education*. London: Routledge.

Pflederer, M. (1964). The responses of children to musical tasks embodying Piaget's principle of conservation. *Journal of Research in Music Education*, 12(4), 251–268.

Piaget, J. (1952). *The Origins of Intelligence in Children* (trans. M. Cook). New York: W. W. Norton and Co.

11 Lev Vygotsky: Learning in Social Contexts

> Learning is more than the acquisition of the ability to think; it is the acquisition of many specialised abilities for thinking about a variety of things.
>
> (Vygotsky, 1978, p. 83)

Lev Vygotsky, a Russian, lived at the same time as Skinner and Piaget, but shortly after his death in 1934 at the early age of 37 his work was blacklisted by the Communist regime. As a result his work did not become widely known until his books had been translated from Russian into English; the first translation was in 1962, but it was later translations that attracted most attention.

Vygotsky's theory represented a major shift away from Piagetian theory. He viewed children's learning and development as a social process in which children learn through interactions with those around them who know more. Termed sociocultural theory, his work focused on how community, family, peer relationships and culture influence children's learning. From the 1980s onwards sociocultural theory emerged as an important framework for understanding the social and cultural complexity of young children's musical lives and learning.

To understand Vygotsky's theory and his ideas on education it is important to appreciate the society in which he lived and the dramatic social and political changes that occurred through his short lifetime. Vygotsky developed his ideas against the backdrop of the Russian Revolution, the First World War and much of the Soviet era under Stalin.

Lev Vygotsky (1896–1934)

Vygotsky was born in Belarus, then part of Russia. Initially he studied medicine and law at Moscow State University and later history and philosophy. He went on to teach in local schools in his hometown. In 1924 he joined the Institute of Psychology in Moscow and completed a PhD in the psychology of art, becoming a lecturer and professor in psychology. He was a prolific writer, producing six books in his last 10 years on aspects of children's cognition. He unfortunately suffered from tuberculosis, the cause of his early death.

DOI: 10.4324/9781003331193-16

Theory

Although Vygotsky was familiar with elements of Skinner's and Piaget's theories of child development, he rejected both their theoretical positions. Instead, in trying to understand how children construct their knowledge, he placed particular emphasis on the social environment and the culture in which learning and cognitive development take place. This emphasis on the social, collective dimension was in keeping with Soviet socialist thinking.

For Vygotsky learning occurs as children interact with people, objects, and events in their everyday environments. Teachers (or a more experienced child or adult) and children work collaboratively to create meaning in ways unique to each child. Children should be offered situations where they will be challenged to discover and work things out for themselves, but where support from more experienced students and teachers is available.

Importantly, in keeping with constructivist thinking, children are active partners in these interactions, constructing their knowledge, skills and attitudes. They are not passively absorbing or mirroring the world around them. However, because their learning is embedded in cultural contexts, there is enormous variation in what they learn and how they learn. The greatest variations might be from culture to culture, but there will be variations at every level including individual family situations and educational contexts.

Vygotsky's theory, interestingly, emphasises the two-way nature of interaction. The social situation does not only impact on children, children also affect their social situation. Imagine an active toddler arriving into a room occupied by adults and it is easy to appreciate how children affect a social situation. By engaging with others around them, children become active members of both their immediate communities – families, childcare settings and so on – and the wider cultural community. The reciprocal nature of this interaction is fundamental to Vygotsky's social constructivism theory.

For Vygotsky social patterns of behaviour and beliefs are passed on to children through the use of 'tools' that are valued in society. By tools he had in mind children's books, toys, nursery rhymes and songs, counting systems, writing systems and more – all the kinds of practices that children engage in at home, in the early childhood setting, school classroom or in the playground. In music, all the resources and symbol systems of music would represent tools. Nowadays tools will also include digital technologies and the media they bring into children's lives from even a very young age. The presence of mobile phones in young children's lives is a good example of a digital cultural tool that children recognise has considerable social value and meaning. They are eager to play with mobile phones, even as babies, and quickly learn how to use them. The media they view typically has music combined with visuals, and so children are absorbing music through everyday experiences.

For Vygotsky language was the most important cultural tool for children's learning. He proposed that through speaking and listening young children develop their ability to understand the world around them. According to Vygotsky children not only express their thinking through talking, their thinking is restructured as it is transformed into speech. Given the blend of music and language in children's early vocalisations, such that it is often impossible to separate the two, Vygotsky's proposition suggests that thinking is also restructured as it is transformed into musical expressions.

Vygotsky disagreed with those who thought that children progress through fixed developmental stages, but equally, he did not think that children could learn anything at any age. He suggested that children's development advances by responding to challenges. Children may see others who are more skilled and try to imitate them. These challenges are self-imposed and children are often highly motivated to copy what they see others do. Equally educators may deliberately pose challenges to children. Importantly the challenges must be well judged. Too difficult and the child may experience stress and frustration. Too easy and the child quickly loses interest. If the new skill or concept is too far outside the child's current capabilities, then no end of support will enable them to grasp it. Children are motivated to progress, and respond positively to challenges. There needs to be just the right balance between challenge and current ability level. That is why, in play, or in learning situations which offer more flexibility, children can contribute to setting their own challenge level.

Vygotsky believed that children can, with help from adults or other children who are more advanced, master concepts, skills and ideas that they cannot understand or achieve on their own. Learning could then lead development. There is a 'zone', as Vygotsky termed it, between the child's current level of development and the point they are capable of reaching under guidance and support. This zone contains skills and concept that are not yet fully developed, but are 'on the edge of emergence' and can emerge if the child is given the right kind of support. This zone is usually termed the zone of proximal development, abbreviated to ZPD. However, the concept of ZPD, often quoted as a key idea of Vygotsky's theory, was, in fact, barely mentioned by Vygotsky. It is interesting to note that other equally important ideas, meanwhile, receive less attention (Gray and MacBlain, 2015).

Key Text

Lev S. Vygotsky. (1978). *Mind in Society: The development of higher psychological processes* (ed. and trans. M. Cole et al.). Cambridge, MA: Harvard University Press.

Internalisation

Vygotsky described children's knowledge acquisition as internalisation. He proposed that every process of the child's learning appears twice: first on the social level between people (interpsychological) and later, on the individual level, inside the child (intrapsychological).

Children may think-talk 'out loud' to make sense. This thinking is then internalised and can be further developed through talking about ideas. Similarly, children may play with music out loud, to make sense of it, and then musical thinking becomes internalised.

Language

Vygotsky suggested that language has two functions. Inner language is used for mental reasoning and external language is used to communicate. Vygotsky suggested that these two forms of language operate separately and that before the age of 2 years a child only uses words socially, they have no internal language. Others disagree and argue that the two forms of language are not so easily separated. Nevertheless the distinction is a useful one. In a similar way, we can think music internally without making a sound, a process some refer to as audiation, and also think music as we perform music.

Intersubjectivity

Each partner adjusts to the perspective of the other, a process termed intersubjectivity. Two or more participants come to an activity or task with different understandings and then arrive at a shared understanding.

The More Knowledgeable/Skilled Other

This might be a parent, teacher, an older sibling or a peer who has greater knowledge and more skills than the learner. Children may observe, imitate or receive specific help from the more knowledgeable other in order to acquire new knowledge and skills.

Enculturation

Children absorb the culture in which they are immersed, a process termed enculturation. Therefore, educators who adopt a sociocultural view of music education believe that the home and community musical experiences which children have already absorbed should form a basis for new learning. They will therefore want to find out about the children's musical backgrounds. At the same time, music educators will want to gradually expand children's musical horizons to include musical experiences beyond what is most familiar to them.

Play and Creativity

For Vygotsky, imaginary play precedes abstract thinking. He proposed that through play children exercise their understanding of objects, develop relationships, imitate adult behaviour and adopt phantasy roles. In many respects, but not all, his ideas on play parallel the work of Piaget. Play is mediated through the nursery rhymes, songs and stories that are part of the child's own culture.

Importantly, however, Vygotsky suggested that children's play is not merely imitation and repetition, but children soon start to elaborate their play with creative and pretend play. They start to become more confident and adventurous and develop rules that they may share with other children. Imaginative play evolves on children's shared understanding of 'the rules' of the game.

Dialogue

Vygotsky emphasised the role of language in cognitive development and how language provides a framework and tools through which children experience, communicate and come to understand.

The most valuable type of talk is 'dialogic' in which the teacher tries to develop ideas initiated by children, by probing and extending them. The teacher may ask challenging questions designed to prompt the children to reflect on their own understanding and thought processes. A dialogic approach leads to genuine understanding because any misunderstandings on the part of the child are revealed and can be re-directed. However this dialogic approach is rare in education, and a closed questioning approach usually prevails. In this style of questioning the educator initiates a question which requires a single, correct answer.

Image of Childhood

Vygotsky's image is the child as an active, sociable member of communities. Children's potential is bound up with the environment of both things and important people around them (adults and other children). They are active producers of their learning through peer interactions and relationships. It follows that such interactions are unique to each child.

Influences on Music Education

The influence of Vygotsky's theory shifted interest to children's experiences of music within their everyday situations at home, in childcare, in the playground, via the media and in community situations such as celebrations and performances. Researchers were interested in what and how children were learning about music in these situations and how that information could then inform educational practice. At the same time, another group of Vygotskian inspired studies looked more closely at the social interactions in educational settings for how those interactions engendered children's learning. Collaborations between children became of interest in paired and group work, as well as the interactions of children with educators. Through this breadth of work it was realised that models of musical development needed to take social and cultural factors into account.

Parents and Child: At Home

One of the first to adopt Vygotsky's theory to explain her observations of young children's musical activity was a Japanese researcher, Mayumi Adachi in the early 1990s (Adachi, 1994). While living with a family in the US that included a pre-school child she observed how the roles adopted by the parents facilitated the musical socialisation of their child at home. She described the parents' roles as transmitter, co-player and practice-partner.

- Transmitter. Musical content (songs, games) was passed from the parent to the child. Later the child, having absorbed it, used the musical content in independent music making.
- Co-player. Parent and child constructed playful situations together.
- Practice partner. The child invited the parents to re-visit and recreate music play situations that had become part of family life so that she could practise.

Children with Children: In Pre-school

In a daycare centre in Sydney, Australia, Peter Whiteman (2001) tracked eight pre-school children and recorded their spontaneous singing during free play approximately once a month over 3 years. This long-term study revealed that the children used songs for specific purposes, that the children are able to co-construct learning from shared experiences and that patterns of musical development were distinctly different for each child. This led him to challenge models of musical development which are closely tied to chronological age. He suggested that conceptions of musical development need to be modified to take into account a range of social contexts and the kinds of music-making processes that occur within those social contexts. He also suggested that much more attention should be given to children's agency in musical situations, their own musical cultures and the roles they can take within those musical cultures. For example, one child may acknowledge another child as being more knowledgeable musically and follow their lead, thus giving that child more agency and a specific role in their musical interactions.

He noticed that children are interested in the music play of other children and learn much from them. As they gain experience at playing musically together, group improvisations may evolve that require musical communication between the group. Out of this synergy, musical ideas emerge. Often these ideas are revisited and refined in group music play.

Teacher and Children: First Years of Schooling

Jackie Wiggins, who has applied Vygotsky's theories in her practice and her research, described children creating collaboratively in school settings. In one example she explained how a teacher of 7-year-olds scaffolded a whole-class song-composing experience. She called the process 'artful scaffolding' because the teacher must apply both musical skills and pedagogical skills (Wiggins, 2015). The children came up with suggestions for some lines of song text that were agreed upon by the whole class. The children started to repeat the words – at first spoken and then quietly chanted – and to sing possible melodies. The teacher, picking up one or two ideas, quietly played a simple chord accompaniment to encourage the children to improvise and to share their ideas within one tonality. Gradually, by listening to one another and the teacher allowing the free, exploratory singing to continue, ideas began to emerge from the class group. The teacher invited individual children to sing their ideas for the whole class to listen. She then asked probing questions designed to prompt evaluation and decision-making by the children. The children continued by suggesting accompanying instruments, ideas for effects to enhance the lyrics, how the song might be sung more expressively and so on. There are interesting similarities between this description of song making and that of Eleanor Smith (see p. 42), working about 100 years previously.

The Theory in Practice

Making music is an inherently social practice, and so there is much of Vygotsky's theory that makes complete sense when applied to musical learning processes. My own book written in 2009 in which I write about music education practice for 3- to 5-year-olds was strongly influenced by Vygotsky's theory and how it can be applied to pedagogical practice. This next example is illustrative of the practice discussed in that book.

Jane is an early childhood educator working in a large, inner-city nursery in central England. She works mostly with the 3- and 4-year-olds. She notices 2 children, outside, playing with small pots of water and sand, mixing the two, and singing a simple chant 'water and sand'. They ask her to help fetch some more water, and as she does this, she sings their chant with slightly changed words 'water for the sand'. They notice her copying their singing, and educator and children start to extend the short phrases into a song with more words, based on their actions. The educator helps the song to take shape by repeating back some phrases.

The small song returns again and again in the days after, as the children play with sand and water, sometimes introduced by Jane, sometimes by the children. The song starts to take on a life of its own. Other children learn the song as it is sung during outdoor play. The words change to fit new play situations. Jane notices one day that a phrase from a children's Disney film song has been incorporated into the song. She is interested to notice how the children's wider, cultural experiences of music become woven into their song.

One day the children are sitting in a circle with a story, and one of them suggests singing 'the sand song' all together.

The educator:

- understands singing to be interwoven in free play, multimodal and sociable, and to be spontaneous, not confined to one formal singing session in the day
- is alert to hearing children's singing play and to joining in with their play
- scaffolds the formation of the song by listening, and repeating back and sometimes extending the song using the original song phrases as the basis
- allows social interactions and peer relationships to contribute to the life of the song
- notices how the song grew from and became part of the children's musical culture, within the small world of their nursery class
- notices how song ideas from the children's musical experiences of the wider musical culture also become reworked into the song
- notices how the song and song ideas took on a life of their own over the course of days and weeks, which ideas were extended and sustained and which were abandoned.

While Vygotsky was interested in language dialogue, music education has extended the idea of dialogue to music made between two or more people: musical dialogues in other words. Musical scaffolding, whether in singing or playing instruments together, can include:

- initiating, by providing a musical beginning that invites continuation
- copying a short musical phrase offered by the child
- expanding a short musical phrase offered by the child or perhaps responding with a musical answer
- reshaping the musical contributions of a child, perhaps by giving the rhythm more definition or singing back the pitches in a more defined tonality
- modelling something new that will be within the child's grasp in order to progress the child within their zone of proximal development
- non-verbal reinforcement, with facial or gestural expression, and
- posing a musical problem, perhaps with a verbal question, and solving it together.

Key Text

Susan Young. (2009). *Music 3–5*. London: Routledge.

Comments and Connections

By the 1980s theories of Dewey, Piaget and Vygotsky had all contributed to the broad perspective of constructivism in educational practice, but with differing emphases. The basic tenet of constructivism – as has been outlined in other sections – is that children bring their existing knowledge and experience into every learning situation as a starting point to which new experiences and information connect. Children construct their understanding, evaluating existing concepts and forming new concepts. There is much overlap between a constructivist and social constructivist classroom. However Vygotsky placed much greater emphasis on learning through social interaction, and on how the cultural environment shapes learning. For Vygotsky, culture provides the child with the cognitive tools needed for development. The teacher's role is to introduce cultural tools as needed to promote, encourage and enhance children's learning.

Vygotsky and Piaget were such important contributors to our understanding of child development and learning that it is informative to put the two theories side by side and then to add implications for music education.

- Vygotsky did not break development down into a series of predetermined stages as did Piaget. Musical development from a Vygotskian perspective is determined by the child's social and cultural experience, it does not proceed in fixed stages.
- Vygotsky suggested that cultural differences can affect development. Piaget's theory suggests that children go through the same universal developmental steps. Music education should take children's home and cultural backgrounds into account.
- Vygotsky believed that all cognitive development happens through social learning and stressed the importance of more knowledgeable adults and peers. Piaget viewed the child as an active, independent problem-solver who acquires knowledge about the world through manipulation and active experimentation. Vygotsky-inspired music pedagogies provide more opportunities for children to play musically in interaction with others (children and adults), rather than explore and discover independently.
- Vygotsky emphasised the role that language plays in learning. Piaget largely ignored the role of language. Music educators need to think how they use verbal language to name, describe and extend children's learning. There are parallels in the way that music is a mode of communication and how musical dialogues and scaffolding can support musical learning.

Translations of Vygotsky's work into English have led to some distortions of his work and to some superficial interpretations. For example, ZPD is only a small element of his work, yet it has become one of the most well-known. Some also suggest that Vygotskian theory places too much emphasis on language and ignores other communication modes and other forms of experiential learning. This may be a very relevant criticism with respect to music education for young children because non-verbal modes of communication – movement, gesture, sound – are central and verbal language probably makes a relatively small contribution until children are older.

Some may criticise constructivism arguing that discovery-based approaches are not effective for all learners, especially very inexperienced learners. Inexperienced learners may lack the necessary first building blocks of learning and may benefit from more structured, direct learning approaches that introduce foundation skills and knowledge. Music educators, for instance, may argue that basic musical skills such as learning to perform rhythms accurately and to sing in tune are learnt through model and imitation processes. In addition, to provide scaffolding and challenging questions tailored to individual children can be difficult to achieve with groups of children.

As a final comment, taking into account children's individual sociocultural situations also poses challenges in practice when working with many children whose backgrounds are very diverse. Calls for the content of music sessions to reflect and connect with the cultural backgrounds of children may in reality be difficult to achieve.

Bibliography

Adachi, M. (1994). The role of the adult in the child's early musical socialization: A Vygotskian perspective. *The Quarterly: Journal of Music Teaching and Learning*, 5 (3), 26–35.

Gray, C. and MacBlain, S. (2015). *Learning Theories in Childhood*. Los Angeles, CA: Sage Publications.

Vygotsky, L. S. (1978). *Mind in Society: The development of higher psychological processes* (ed. and trans. M. Cole et al.). Cambridge, MA: Harvard University Press.

Wiggins, J. (2015). *Teaching for Musical Understanding*, 3rd edition. Oxford: Oxford University Press.

Whiteman, P. (2001). How the bananas got their pyjamas: A study of the metamorphosis of preschoolers' spontaneous singing as viewed through Vygotsky's Zone of Proximal Development. Unpublished thesis submitted to the University of New South Wales in partial fulfilment of the requirements for the degree Doctor of Philosophy.

12 Jerome Bruner: Processes of Learning

> The first object of any act of learning – is that it should serve us in the future. Learning should not only take us somewhere; it should allow us later to go further more easily.
>
> (Bruner, 1960, p. 17)

Jerome Bruner (1915–2016) was an American psychologist whose work has made a major contribution to our understanding of the processes of learning and teaching. He was one of the original founders of the cognitive revolution that changed the direction of psychology when it was, at the time, dominated by behaviourist theories. A major theme in Bruner's theory is that learning is an active process in which children construct new concepts based upon their current and/or past knowledge. This core idea of constructivism may be easily accepted now, but at the time it contradicted the dominant behaviourist thinking.

Bruner was especially interested in how teachers should structure learning and two major ideas, the modes through which children represent their thinking and the idea of spiral curriculum have been of particular value to music education. From the mid-1960s onwards his theories were directly applied by some music educators, particularly in the US.

Jerome Bruner (1915–2016)

Born in New York, Bruner was a psychologist who also became a key figure in the field of education. He had a long and illustrious career teaching at the universities of Harvard, Oxford and New York. In 1960 he co-founded the Center for Cognitive Studies at Harvard. In England he led the Oxford Preschool research project from 1975–1980. In the late 1990s he became very interested in the pre-schools of Reggio Emilia (see p. 131). Over the span of his career his theoretical thinking developed, gradually moving from a cognitive studies position to a cultural psychological position.

DOI: 10.4324/9781003331193-17

Theory

Bruner emphasised the importance of teaching children the fundamental conceptual structure of a subject over simple facts or skills. According to Bruner, having a conceptual structure enables children to select information from their experiences, to organise that information, transform it and to construct new concepts. Children can thus take a more active, self-guided role in their own learning.

One of the most influential aspects of his work – and one that has been especially useful for early childhood music education – is the idea that children use three modes of representing, or symbolising, human thought: enactive, iconic and symbolic.

Enactive

A child learns about the world through actions on physical objects and the outcomes of these actions. Enactive knowledge is non-verbal.

> *A baby takes an egg shaker, shakes it, discovers the sound it makes and is attracted to the sound. The movement to create the sound becomes encoded through memory, as kinaesthetic memory (muscle memory). The child's concept of egg shaker is therefore a blend of the sound with the feel of holding and shaking the egg shaker. In the enactive mode, the concept of egg shaker remains fixed on the actual object; there is no transfer or connections with other objects or concepts.*

Iconic

The iconic mode depends on perceptual organisation and imagery – sound (aural), movement (kinaesthetic) and visual (imagery). Children might be presented with models, images or pictures to support their learning.

> *Seeing an egg shaker picture in a book, the child may recognise it, point and make a gesture to shake it. This means that children can now think about objects that are not actually present. It is a stage of internalisation. But the images are still limited by the characteristics of the egg shaker, its shape, colour, size and so on. The image cannot capture higher order concepts such as the nature of the sound, the timbre or different ways of playing it.*

Symbolic

In the symbolic mode the child is developing the ability to think in abstract terms. Thinking in music can take place through language and visual systems. Certain images and/or words can stand in for an idea or object.

> An older child can now talk about the egg shaker in words, describing the sound, understanding instructions to play the egg shaker in certain ways or being able to describe how they are playing it. They could be shown how to read simple notation systems. Not all learning can be converted into symbolic understanding – for example, some expressive, creative ideas may defy conversion into words or symbols.

According to Bruner, when the child is faced with new knowledge a combination of concrete (enactive), pictorial (iconic) and symbolic activities will lead to more effective learning. The modes of representation are integrated and only loosely sequential as they merge and translate into each other. He was especially interested in how information is represented through symbols and words and how these representations enable children to make connections between concepts.

These theoretical ideas suggest that the educator should translate learning experiences from mode to mode, giving thought to which mode or modes are appropriate to the child's current state of understanding. In this way cross-modal experience strengthens children's ability to build conceptual understanding.

Scaffolding

Bruner was very interested in Vygotsky's ideas about the zone of proximal development and in the idea of scaffolding. As a psychologist interested in early child development, he observed mothers interacting with their babies and explained the role of the mother. He wrote, 'in such instances, mothers most often see their role as supporting the child in achieving the intended outcome, entering only to assist or reciprocate or "scaffold" the action' (Bruner, 1975, p. 12).

Thus scaffolding refers to the process by which adults (or other children who are more capable) provide support for a child by offering guidance and help. Importantly scaffolding should be judged to be just what the child needs at that moment in terms of quantity, timing and type of support. For instance, a mother may notice that her baby is trying to reach for a drum, push it within her sitting baby's reach, and then hold it at an angle so that he can tap it successfully. A toddler might be able to crawl to the drum, but need help tilting it to play. An educator might notice that an older child would benefit from being given a beater and shown how to hold it, so that she can strike the drum more successfully. Scaffolding must constantly adjust to the needs of the learner so that the learner can become independent and the adult gradually redundant.

However, crucially, what is being scaffolded is not just success with the task but also the gradual development of the child's thinking about and understanding of the task. Scaffolding shows the child how to do the task, step by step, how to break it down and how to sequence the parts of the activity in order to complete it. Children who can talk are encouraged to talk about the steps to achieve the task. So the teacher both shows and explains, 'if you hold the beater like this, the drum like this and strike in the centre, you will make a good sound.' Teaching, said Bruner, is greatly facilitated by language. The aim is to develop children's independent thinking and how we use talk, as a teacher, plays a key role that process.

The Spiral Curriculum

The spiral curriculum was based on Bruner's philosophy that children can be taught any topic at any age if they are introduced to the essential information and fundamental concepts of that topic in an age-appropriate way. Spiral curriculum planning begins by breaking down skills or knowledge to the most fundamental concept or basic skill. The planning then enables children to revisit those concepts and skills in ever increasing depth and complexity as they mature. As children gather experience they should be able to transfer conceptual understanding and skills to new areas.

Importantly Bruner argued that children should discover the underlying structure of the topic for themselves and find the links and relationships between different concepts and facts, rather than simply being told or imitating a model. So, for example, in starting to learn about rhythmic patterning, the children are given opportunities to explore rhythm patterns and their explorations are supported by translations into visual and verbal representations. The teacher seeks to guide them in grasping the underpinning concepts, for example, pattern, accent, twice as fast, twice as slow, or how to find the beat that underpins rhythm patterning.

Learning as Culture-Dependent

Bruner evolved his theories over a long period and later in his career he became interested in how children show a strong predisposition to culture, meaning that they are very interested in what their parents, their siblings and peers do and with no prompting, try to imitate what they observe around them. Later in his career, he became critical of the so-called cognitive revolution because it had evolved to become too focused on the mind as a kind of information processor. He moved in a different theoretical direction and began to frame his work within cultural psychology. This interest in the cultural dimension of learning was reflected in his 1996 book, *The Culture of Education*. In this book he discussed how children construct their understandings based on common cultural themes, ideas, symbols, beliefs and values and the idea that knowledge is intersubjective – that is, it emerges through social interaction. Thus, learning is a process of shared meaning making; an idea that is fruitful for music education given that music gains its structure and meaningfulness by being shared between people.

Another basic principle of cultural psychology is that there are essentially two ways by which we organise and manage our knowledge of the world: paradigmatic and narrative thinking.

Paradigmatic and Narrative Thought

For Bruner, paradigmatic though is orderly and logical and can be judged to be correct or true. Piaget's theory emphasises this type of logical thought. In contrast, narrative thought is looser, based more on images and can be interpreted in many ways. Creative explorations in music, drama, literature and other forms of story-telling would constitute narrative thought. Narrative play and thinking opens up creative possibilities. However education traditionally prioritises paradigmatic thought and treats the narrative arts — song, drama, fiction and theatre — as marginal and as less necessary.

Image of Childhood

Bruner viewed the child as having a natural curiosity and desire to become competent and as having the capacity to become autonomous learners, who have 'learnt how to learn'. In later life he became closely involved in the work of the nursery schools of Reggio Emilia and he was in tune with the strong image of competent and active childhood held by Malaguzzi and his colleagues (see p. 132).

Key Texts

Jerome Bruner. (1960). *The Process of Education*. Cambridge, MA: Harvard University Press.
Jerome Bruner. (1986). *Actual Minds: Possible worlds*. Cambridge, MA: Harvard University Press.

Influences on Music Education

Bruner's work was more closely related to educational practice than the work of some other psychologists discussed in this book. He was especially interested in curriculum structure and in the processes of learning and teaching and these ideas have proved to be very useful to music education. In comparison Piaget and Vygotsky's work inspired research which sought to understand children's learning processes and development which could then, in a further step, be applied to educational practice. Bruner's ideas were first taken up by music educators in the US, notably Eunice Boardman and Barbara Andress.

Eunice Boardman

Drawing on Bruner's ideas, Eunice Boardman developed what she called a *Generative Theory of Musical Learning* (1988). This underpinned a curriculum series that started with kindergarten and continued through primary (elementary grades) which she co-authored through several editions from 1966–1988. Learning she wrote, 'is the construction of meaning, a selection, retention and transformation that recognises all learning is holistic, a fusion of action, cognition and emotion' (Boardman, 1988, p. 4). Children learn actions (specific motor skills and music behaviours) that are formed and guided by particular thinking skills (cognitive operations) because our emotions (dispositions, values, feelings, beliefs) interpret these actions as meaningful. She emphasised that learning takes place in a sociocultural context that influences and moulds the direction the learning process will take. She wanted children to come to understand the significance of music as a personal mode of expression.

The curriculum series focused on the learning of musical concepts which are re-visited multiple times, in a spiral curriculum structure, until the child grasps a full understanding of the concept. Children, she explained, should grasp the conceptual structure of music so that many other aspects can be related to that structure in meaningful ways. Bruner's theory also inspired the progression from enactive to iconic to symbolic expression in her co-writing of the series. She followed the following principles.

- Music learning is a holistic experience. She recommended a sequence of 'whole-part-whole'. The whole piece of music, or the song, is the starting point. The focus may then turn to a part or an element, within the whole, to focus children's learning. Then there should be a return to the whole music experience.
- Music is a way of representing our experience and symbols (notations, words, syllables, movements) help to represent the music. The way that these symbol systems are used shapes the way children come to understand music.
- What children learn should give them the means and the basis on which they can learn more. This is what Boardman meant by a 'generative' theory of learning. Learning follows a spiral that moves ever upwards, but also swings outwards and inwards, sometimes gathering in more, sometimes focusing back in on detail.

Boardman emphasised the value of a learning environment in which children 'moved from a known through an unknown to a new known' (Boardman, 1988). She outlined six components of the learning environment:

1. Content: the musical concept that will be the focus, but it must be contained within a whole music experience (not separated out).

2   Context: the music (songs and music to perform, music for listening). Boardman stated that the musical examples should be representative of diverse cultures and times, be drawn from a variety of genres, be appropriate for the learner and of aesthetic value.
3   Musical behaviour: how the children will engage in the music; performing, listening, describing and creating. Children should be involved in constantly evolving cycles of these different types of musical behaviour.
4   Mode of knowledge representation: the three ways that a learner can communicate understanding: enactively, iconically and symbolically.
5   Cognitive skills: the way that the first four components interact and how the learner moves from a known through an unknown to a new known. For Boardman learning involves the fusion of emotion, cognition and action.
6   Positive attitude: the learning environment, allowing for delight and personal expression in making music.

Concepts

Boardman (with Bergethon) explained the process of forming musical concepts (Boardman and Bergethon, 1979, pp. 11–12). Concepts enable children to generalise, to categorise certain groups of musical objects, qualities or the relationships between things, and to differentiate. Children can then apply concepts in new situations, so that they can work with ideas, be creative and solve problems.

- Concept formation depends on perception. Children need to be able to perceive the characteristics of a concept. When the characteristics are experienced in a direct and sensory way – by moving, by seeing, by hearing, by touching – concept formation occurs more easily. In music learning, therefore, this suggests that children should have plenty of opportunities to experience music aurally, visually and in body movement.
- Concept formation moves from the concrete to the abstract. Many musical concepts are abstract and so their introduction must be planned around the use of materials and activities that provide the children with concrete, hands-on, sensory experience. Children can form concepts more easily if they are related to broader concepts the children already possess – so tempo may be related to the children's experiences of speed, or dynamics related to children's everyday experiences of sound.
- Concept formation depends on the example. Children's ability to form concepts is related to how complex the example is. On the other hand, over-simplified examples – e.g. playing a drum beat to represent steady beat – may not be genuinely musical. Music is a highly complex art and melodic and rhythmic concepts should be interwoven into whole music experiences. The musical examples the teacher selects for teaching musical concepts will, therefore, require careful thought.

- Concept formation depends on past experience. Children need to have a firm grasp of foundational concepts before they can move on to more complex ones.
- Concept formation is a gradual process. Secure concept formation is a long, slow process that moves from vague understanding to more precise. Children will need many similar experiences to develop musical understanding and they will need to revisit concepts over time, in new musical experiences. Learning the correct musical vocabulary accompanies the development of concepts, but as a follow-on process, not a leading process. Children need the vocabulary in order to be able to discuss and communicate their musical ideas.

The following list summarises categories of concepts (Boardman and Bergethon, 1979, pp. 5–6):

- Concepts of rhythmic organisation: beat, accent groupings, rhythm pattern, rhythm of the melody.
- Concepts of melodic organisation: up-down-same, step-skip-same, range, tonal organisation.
- Concepts of harmonic organisation: multiple sounds, rest-unrest, texture.
- Concepts of formal organisation: motif, phrase, repetition-contrast.
- Concepts of expressive organisation: These are communicated through the organisation of melody, rhythm, harmony, tempo, dynamics and tone colour within the musical whole.
- Concepts of stylistic organisation: Style may refer to music of different cultures, periods, or composers, as well as types and methods of composition.

Key Reading

Eunice Boardman (1988). The generative theory of musical learning, part 1: Introduction. *General Music Today*, 2(1), 4–5.

The Theory in Practice

A large section of a book titled *Music and Young Children* (1969) by Frances Aronoff describes music learning experiences for young children that are based on a combination of Dalcroze principles and Bruner's theory. Most of these experiences begin with a song which provides the children with opportunities to encounter different concepts of music, in enactive and iconic representations and in translations from one mode to another. In this book she has scripted imaginary conversations between teacher and children in order to illustrate her pedagogical approach – an approach that emphasises dialogue between children and teacher. The teacher takes ideas from the children, scaffolds their learning and guides them towards clear learning goals based on musical concepts. She describes this process, stating that the teacher must 'follow along, ahead of the children'; ahead in guiding the dynamic interaction of the session toward the stated goals.

The descriptions in her book are wordy and there are many of them. This is a trimmed-down version of one.

CHILDREN: You said we could sing Ritsch Ratsch for everybody – the song we sang in the play yard. Help us.
TEACHER: Yes, I will. What did we hear this morning that made us think of the song earlier?
CHILDREN: When I was pushing M. in the swing you sang it. And when the empty swing was twisting [child demonstrates].
TEACHER: [to all the children] Can you try moving like that? How is she moving?
CHILDREN: Her arms are up, they are the ropes of the swing. Her feet are still.
TEACHER: Everybody twist and sing. – Now what else can we do with this song?
CHILDREN: Push the swing. First you push, then you pull.
TEACHER: Good, push and pull – anything you like. And sing. Notice how A. makes his whole body help his arms. He pushes hard. He must be pushing something heavy. Everyone do it like A. What happens to our song when we push like that?
CHILDREN: It's slow and heavy. It's loud. [lots of answers]
TEACHER: It's slow and loud. What will you do when I sing the song this way? [sings very fast, softly] And this way? [slowly and very softly]

(Aronoff, 1969, p. 98, précised)

In this lesson script she illustrates how learners will progress from the known, through an unknown to a new known. The teacher:

- starts from the interests of children and their everyday experience and seeks their full involvement, with whole body movement, motivations and feelings
- identifies, in the moment, what musical learning can emerge from their initiating interests
- provides a song or instrumental pattern to which the children move so that they experience the musical concept in movement (enactive)
- takes the children's ideas for movement, developing them through visual imagery (iconic)
- asks the children to explain the musical concept in words (symbolic) and extracts the musical terms from their answers and reinforces those terms, and
- challenges the children to demonstrate their understanding of the musical concept in new musical experiences.

Concepts of music for Aronoff are the separate elements of music in their simplest form – rhythm, tempo, melody, tone quality, dynamics, design (form) and texture. She emphasises that the acquisition of concepts, particularly in the early years, requires planning of learning that is based on a structure of the elements of music. The teacher should then identify which concepts are inbuilt in the songs or other musical materials to be used, and then consider how these concepts can be represented in the child's body movement (enactive mode). Her model of planning always starts with a whole song or whole piece of music which then leads to some form of focus on smaller parts to encourage children to grasp musical concepts, and then returns to a whole music experience: the whole-part-whole sequence. Also important to Aronoff is the concern for children's affective experience that blends with cognitive growth. Ideas, she writes, are not normally isolated from emotional experience (Aronoff, 1969, p. 8).

The teacher has a clear learning goal in mind yet seeks to allow the children to pursue their own lines of thinking. She writes:

> it should be clear that a rigid lesson plan is inappropriate and inadequate to the challenge of beginning where the child is (experientially and physically), encouraging his exploration of movement and image. Yet use of the concept checklist gives focus and purpose to procedures typified by flexibility and originality. This guided yet free approach can be an efficient and effective means of helping the child to learn what music is all about and to prepare him to enjoy it ...
> (Aronoff, 1969, p. 67)

She recommends that children should encounter these elements in a broad range of music, from sixth-century plainsong to contemporary music of all types. The concepts should also be highly varied, for example, melody can include chromatic, atonal as well as tonal relationship and rhythmic patterns should be metred, syncopated or free, following speech or movement patterns. Echoing Bruner, she is clear that children can experience musical complexity at any age if the experiences are presented in a way that is appropriate to the children. Note how this principle contrasts with the idea of recapitulation that underpins the methods of Kodály and Orff – that young children need musical simplicity. Note too that her emphasis on bodily movement is as a mode of enactive learning, not rhythm as a 'primitive' musical foundation.

Key Text

Frances Webber Aronoff. (1969). *Music and Young Children*. New York: Holt, Rinehart and Winston.

Comments and Connections

Bruner, as did Vygotsky, emphasised the social nature of learning. Both agreed that adults should play an active role in assisting the child's learning by scaffolding. This emphasis on learning as an interactive process contrasts with theories of learning which emphasise independent exploration and children discovering for themselves. In Marjorie Glynne-Jones's book her Piagetian perspective encouraged her to stand back, describe and analyse what the children are doing, rather than suggest how to engage and scaffold. Aronoff in contrast, through her wordy scripts, attempts to convey the process of teaching as interactive dialogue. In this process the teacher tries to both elicit the children's ideas and at the same time to be one step ahead of the children and guiding their learning. Dewey also emphasised the importance of starting with the children's interests and the teacher then bridging the gap between children's interests and the learning content of the curriculum. Aronoff illustrates this process of bridging-the-gap in her explanations of practice.

Aronoff's and Boardman's emphasis on the fusion of emotion, cognition and action echoes Susan Isaacs' conviction that learning should be holistic. Susan Isaacs, as did Boardman and Aronoff, proposed that authentic learning requires emotional engagement; the joy of music.

Bruner's work also suggests that a learner, even at a very young age, is capable of learning any concept as long as the pedagogical strategy is appropriate the child's capabilities. This is in contrast to Piaget and other stage theorists who believed educators should wait until children were at a stage of maturity when they were ready for certain types of learning. For Bruner, as with Vygotsky, it was experience that drove development rather than biological maturation. Aronoff agrees and explains how the translation from one to another mode drives cognitive growth. In this respect she credits Dalcroze for intuitively understanding these principles in his philosophy of music education. Knowing through movement and the perception of aural imagery connects Bruner's theory to the work of Jaques-Dalcroze and his followers.

One of the implications of the spiral curriculum and scaffolding children's learning, as illustrated through the example from Aronoff's book, is that the teacher needs to have a thorough knowledge of what is being taught. Superficial knowledge of music is not sufficient to understand the core concepts and essential information, to make the planning decisions and to provide the range of support that different children may require. Musical scaffolding – to play with children musically and to scaffold their music-making – requires in-the-moment music decision making that combines musical and pedagogical skills.

Some suggest that it is not appropriate to intervene and scaffold young children all the time; that they need exploratory learning and to be left to their own devices. Learning through play allows children to expand the possibilities; teachers might intervene and inadvertently close down children's ideas. Scaffolding therefore lends itself to some situations and types of learning better than others. Aronoff's work illustrates how to work with a class of children and develop a dialogic approach in which children can contribute their own ideas, even if the final direction of learning is being guided by the teacher.

Bibliography

Aronoff, F. W. (1969). *Music and Young Children*. New York: Holt, Rinehart and Winston.

Boardman, E. (1988). The generative theory of musical learning: Part 1—Introduction. *General Music Today*, 2(1), 4–5.

Boardman, E. and Bergethon, B. (1979). *Musical Growth in the Elementary School, Fourth Edition*. New York: Holt, Rinehart and Winston.

Bruner, J. S. (1960). *The Process of Education*. Cambridge, MA: Harvard University Press.

Bruner, J. S. (1975). From communication to language: A psychological perspective. *Cognition*, 3(3), 255–287.

Bruner, J. S. (1996). *Culture of Education*. Cambridge, MA: Harvard University Press.

Part V

Part V includes philosophies, theories and pedagogical approaches that have influenced the directions of practice in more recent years, although some of the approaches have roots reaching back into the last century.

The varied nature of these final sections reflects the philosophical and theoretical diversity that has come to be characteristic of more recent music education thinking. Here there are theoretical influences from many directions, including sociology, ethnomusicology, contemporary musicology, theories of learning through play and advances in infant psychology. Such is the diversity of ideas that three of the five sections cover broad trends rather than home in on a single theorist or philosophy. One trend is captured in a section on musical play, another on listening and exploring sound, and another that addresses issues of diversity and tracks the progression from multiculturalism to decolonisation. Two sections, one on the practice approach known as Reggio Emilia and another on communicative musicality, present more compact topics.

Research with babies, starting in the 1970s onwards contradicted earlier assumptions that babies lived in a world of perceptual confusion and revealed just how competent they are. Interpretations of babies' abilities to interact with others in ways broadly defined as musical has provided an important stimulus to recent work in early childhood music education, particularly with under-3-year-olds.

These more recent influences from sociology, anthropology, ethnomusicology and cultural studies, including childhood studies, underscore the need for music educators to understand how the context, the content, the processes of music and the processes of learning and teaching in music are inextricably inter-related. At the turn of the twenty-first century, early childhood music education could no longer be viewed as narrowly informed by the philosophies of the grand methods, or psychological theories of how children learn but started to take account of the social and cultural worlds inhabited by children and their families. This realigning of music education brings the teaching of music closer to the realities of young children's and families' everyday lives, and more involved and concerned with the issues raised by those realities.

DOI: 10.4324/9781003331193-18

13 Loris Malaguzzi and Reggio Emilia

The child has
A hundred languages
A hundred hands
A hundred thoughts
A hundred ways of thinking, of playing, of speaking ...
                    (Malaguzzi, 1996, p. 3)

The Reggio Emilia approach is an educational philosophy closely tied to pedagogical theory that originated in the nursery schools of Reggio Emilia, a town in northern Italy. Loris Malaguzzi was the central figure who inspired the educational philosophy. He championed children's rights in education, the idea of 'a hundred languages' and a positive image of young children as competent and agentic.

The Reggio Emilia pre-schools evolved a pedagogical approach based on encouraging imaginative thinking, listening to children, documentation of learning processes, community involvement, democracy and professional dialogue. The approach has been influential on early childhood practice world-wide and has also influenced the work of some early childhood music educators.

It is valuable to understand the origins of the Reggio Emilia approach within the context of the time. The Second World War was over and Italy was reeling from the aftermath. In the small city of Reggio Emilia a community of women were rebuilding their lives, their community and their schools. The women were determined to create a good pre-school system that would encourage their children to think independently, critically and to work collaboratively so that a future generation could never again allow a fascist regime to take hold. The parents and teachers wanted publicly funded schools open to all families in the community. Appreciating the origins of the distinctive practice that evolved in Reggio Emilia nursery schools is a reminder that early childhood education is inherently political and that it is vital to define the core educational values and vision.

Loris Malaguzzi (1920–1994)

Loris Malaguzzi came to Reggio Emilia as a young volunteer teacher in 1946 and stayed until his death in 1994, providing leadership to the development of the pedagogical approach. He had completed degrees in pedagogy and psychology and took inspiration from philosophers and theorists such as Dewey, Piaget, Vygotsky and Bruner.

Key Text

Loris Malaguzzi. (1996). *The Hundred Languages of Children: The Reggio Emilia approach to early childhood education.* Norwood, NJ: Ablex Publishing Corporation.

Image of the Child

The image of the child that underpins the pedagogy is central to the Reggio Emilia philosophy and is made explicit. Children are viewed as competent and strong in potential for learning. They are seen as individuals who are curious about their world and active in constructing knowledge as they interact with the environment and with others; their peers, their parents and teachers.

Early childhood is considered to be a crucial stage in a child's life because it is the time when they make sense of their world through active interaction with it. It is not viewed as merely a stage to be passed through or preparation for what comes later. This contrast between early childhood as 'being' rather than 'becoming' has become an established theme in early childhood education theory, partly through the influence of Reggio Emilia pedagogical philosophy.

The Principles

There is no single defined Reggio theory or philosophy but a number of principles that shape practice. The Reggio approach is primarily constructivist. The child is viewed as being an active constructor of knowledge rather than a passive receiver of knowledge. The curriculum emerges from the children's own interests and these interests are identified through the educator observing, documenting and talking with children. This pedagogical approach is often described as the child and adult researching together. Children follow their own interests, but within a framework that is guided and supported by the educators. Importantly the educators do not start with fixed activities or learning content in mind. They do, however, prompt the children's learning, usually by providing initial stimuli (often called provocations) that are intended to capture the children's interests and imaginations. They then guide the children's activities in directions they think will be fruitful for children's learning. This process is described as a two-way dialogue between children and educators.

The Environment

The environment is considered to be the third teacher. The space and the things in that space are understood to motivate, support and engender the learning experiences and ideas of the children. Space also fosters social relationships and collaboration. There should be order and beauty in the environment and so it is considered important that the design of the buildings and the interior arrangements of furniture, objects and displays are visually pleasing.

A Pedagogy of Listening

The educators of Reggio Emilia nursery schools have evolved what they call a 'pedagogy of listening'. This is a broad concept of listening that involves giving attention to the children beyond simply hearing sound. It emphasises multiple listening, or listening not just with ears, but with all senses (sight, touch, smell, taste, orientation). To listen requires being present in the here and now, focussed and open to seeing the possibilities. The pedagogy of listening also includes 'visible listening' through the documentation and interpretation of children's learning.

The Role of the Educator

The teacher's role within the Reggio Emilia approach is complex. The educator is seen as a collaborator and guide, someone who learns alongside the children, rather than someone who leads and instructs. Educators and children explore the learning experiences together; they 'research' in partnership. Adults observe, listen and actively engage in processes of open-ended discovery and problem-solving alongside the children. Their role is to present challenges and provoke ideas, sometimes by introducing conflicting ideas. The adults organise the materials and media to guide the children in making thoughtful decisions.

Documentation

A central feature of the Reggio Emilia pedagogy is documentation. Children's work, their ideas and their thought processes are documented. Documentation may take a variety of different forms; written descriptions, transcripts of children's talk, drawings, photos, video clips or 3D media such as models and clay. This documentation forms the basis of later reflective discussions in which the educators analyse and try to understand the children's learning processes. From these shared discussions, they decide on next steps and how to guide the children's learning. Documentation is a process of making the children's learning visible and is also a process through which the children's learning can be revisited and evaluated. It is central as a means for ensuring the work is tied to the children's interests and that the pedagogy remains inspiring and innovative.

Educators, who usually work in pairs, are given non-contact time away from the children to review documentation, discuss and plan collaboratively. Continuous professional development through the process of documentation and reflection is a high priority.

Emergent Curriculum, Provocations and Project Work

The curriculum is not fixed in advance, but emerges, based on the educators' observations of children's interests and listening to the children's ideas and discussions. The educators may introduce provocations – an event, or objects that are intended to stimulate interest and curiosity. Through observing and talking with children, educators try to gain insight into children's ideas and thinking processes. Projects emerge, building on these interests. Projects may extend for many weeks or peter out after a short while, depending on the level of the children's engagement.

The Hundred Languages

Children are considered to have many languages – the hundred languages – through which they express themselves and communicate their thoughts and ideas: words, movement, drawing, painting, singing, dancing, storytelling, shadow play, modelling, sounds are just a few examples. All these languages are of equal value and should be supported in giving representation and meaning to the children's learning. In this way children are able to explore many different ways of expressing themselves. They strengthen their learning in projects by exploring the connections and links between the different languages.

Atelier (Workshop) and Artist

The early childhood centres have a workshop, an atelier, in which a wide variety of materials are available for exploration and creative activities. In Reggio Emilia nurseries, the atelierista, the name given to the artist who works in the atelier, usually has a background in visual arts and works closely with the educators.

Collaboration, Dialogue and Relationships

Children are understood to be members of a school, a family and a community and to learn through interaction with their friends, siblings, parents, educators, objects and cultural symbols. Collaboration involving the negotiation of ideas is seen as essential to furthering children's cognitive development. Children are encouraged to work together to problem-solve; talking to one another, negotiating and deciding. The balance for each child between a sense of belonging to the group and a sense of individual self is considered important and is managed through this dialogue and negotiation.

Parents are closely involved in the nursery schools and information between parents and educators is two-way, so that educators come to understand the children's home life and parents understand their children's nursery school experiences. Parents may join in with children's activities. Early childhood education is seen as a system of relationships embedded in wider social and cultural systems. At heart, education from the Reggio Emilia perspective is understood to have a political purpose and that purpose is to foster democracy (reflecting its origins).

The Philosophy in Practice

The Reggio Emilia approach is first and foremost a philosophy of education that has given rise to a set of pedagogical principles. Some music education projects have adopted and adapted the pedagogical principles to music. The Sight-Lines Initiative is a UK organisation that promotes and supports creative practice based on Reggio principles. One strand of their activity has focused on the potential of musicality as a language of expression. This description is taken from a Sight-Lines project named 'The Sounds of Leaping' (2009):

> We observed that a group of children were interested in jumping from 'rocket' towers outside. Together with the children we constructed a project exploring how they could compose music expressing their movement ideas. The children took the lead in exploring and composing their own music, and we acted on new ideas from them throughout the project, for example when they wanted to work with new movements and instruments. We enabled two of the children to become leaders, and work with younger children to explore these ideas. We worked with the children to create a film of their movements, to which the group composed their own musical soundtrack. The children made crucial editorial decisions to create the film, supported by the staff and music leader. At the end of the project they presented their work to other children in school and to parents.

The educators:

- observed an interest initiated by the children
- introduced the idea of making music to express movement
- allowed the children to lead the music explorations and supported and enabled their ideas

- worked with the children to create a film, and
- presented the work to an audience.

Music Workshop

The inclusion of a workshop, the atelier, in Reggio Emilia nurseries – a dedicated space in which the children's artistic explorations are supported by a professional artist – has inspired musician Wendell Hanna, working in the US, to set up a music workshop environment. She has written about her music workshop approach in early childhood settings.

Key Text

Wendell Hanna., (2017). *The Children's Music Studio: A Reggio-inspired approach.* Oxford: Oxford University Press.

Comments and Connections

The education offered in the pre-schools of Reggio Emilia cannot be exactly replicated outside of Italy in other countries because the approach has evolved within that particular social and historical context, the educational infrastructure and the wider community. However, the principles have been and continue to be very inspiring to educators internationally. They provide a model of education that stimulates educators to ask fundamental questions about their values, aims, image of childhood and pedagogical strategies. For music educators, it is valuable to see how a Reggio Emilia inspired education takes children's creative and artistic work seriously. In addition, some of the pedagogical techniques can be adopted directly for music education, for example, the pedagogy of listening and the practice of documentation.

The central role given to the visual arts through the atelieresta means that, in the Reggio Emilia pre-schools, arts based on other media, sound and movement for example, may be less well developed. In 1998, Barbara Andress wrote an article asking, 'Where's the music [in the Reggio Emilia approach]?', pointing out that music seems to receive less attention than visual arts. There have, nevertheless, been some projects that have focussed on how to apply Reggio Emilia principles to music education, both in Italy and internationally. Some of the most successful projects have assumed a multi-modal approach in which sounds and rhythms are but one component of blended mixed media activity.

For music education, there may be tensions between the conventional, and expected ways of providing music education and the Reggio Emilia approach. For educators used to delivering a ready-made programme of content and activities that are led by the adult, the pedagogical principles represent a radical change. There can be a misunderstanding that Reggio Emilia is a child-centred pedagogy that encourages free play without restraint. However, that is to misunderstand the principle that learning directions are emergent, based on the children's motivations and interests. Those unfamiliar with the pedagogy may, at first, find the educator role complex and unclear, especially understanding the centrality of documentation, and may find it challenges some conceptions of their competence as music educators.

The emphasis on observation, diagnosing children's learning needs and then prompting their learning has much in common with the approach of Maria Montessori, also originating in Italy. But where Montessori focussed on independent learning, Reggio Emilia focuses on collaborative learning and dialogue. Montessori materials are a constant and structured part of the environment with a learning aim embedded in their structure. In contrast Reggio Emilia provocations might take any form and are more flexible and open-ended. The pedagogical style of Montessori is more directive whereas Reggio Emilia educators seek to understand the children's intentions and build on them.

The pedagogy of Reggio Emilia often begins with provocations that focus on materials and exploring their potentials. In the case of music, the basic materials are sounds and objects that produce sound. As a result, the work that evolves can have similarities with the approaches described in two following sections; one about sound and listening, and another about musical play.

One of the challenges of the Reggio Emilia approach is to allow for children's individual participation and responses, and then coordinate the different needs, interests and abilities of a group of children. Quite simply, music makes a noise and the noise of one child can interfere with the sounds of another child. The educators must be confident in their ability to navigate the activities and develop them with the children in interesting and meaningful ways. Educators working in pairs or even teams, rather than individually, may find it easier to put the pedagogical principles into action.

The process of documentation can also be challenging for music educators to put into practice. Documenting musical activity usually requires some use of audio and/or video recording and this can be difficult to manage in the flow of children's activity. Moreover educators may be working with many children across a week and may have little or no time that allows for the process of reviewing documentation and forward planning, particularly if it involves reviewing recordings.

Together, the early childhood education community of Reggio Emilia developed an approach that has theoretical kinship with many theories, in particular those of Dewey, Montessori, Piaget, Vygotsky and Bruner. Bruner and Vygotsky's recognition of how children have capacities for problem solving and how children are embedded within a social and cultural environment are in tune with Malaguzzi's ideas. Bruner found such affinity between his evolving theories of cultural education and the practice of Reggio Emilia that in the 1990s he visited and worked with the Reggio Emilia nurseries.

Bibliography

Andress, B. (1998). Where's the music in 'The hundred languages of children'? *General Music Today*, 11(3),14–17.

Malaguzzi, L. (1996). *The Hundred Languages of Children: The Reggio Emilia approach to early childhood education*. Norwood, NJ: Ablex Publishing Corporation.

14 Listening and Exploring Sound

> Today all sounds belong to a continuous field of possibilities lying within the comprehensive dominion of music. Behold the new orchestra: the sonic universe! And the musicians: anyone and anything that sounds!
>
> (Schafer, 1994, p. 5)

This section does not focus on one theorist or one method but draws together various theories and pedagogical ideas that share a focus on listening and exploring sound. These pedagogical ideas have tended to come and go, drawing on different philosophies and motivations over the years. They have not coalesced into one defined approach but nevertheless have much in common.

These approaches emphasise:

- listening attentively and with sensitivity to sounds
- listening to sounds for their own sake, specifically the intrinsic qualities of sounds
- fostering an interest in environmental sounds, becoming aware of soundscapes
- exploring sounds that children can make with their voices, their bodies, with objects and musical instruments
- using sounds creatively
- expanding listening experiences to music children might not otherwise encounter, in particular experimental music, and
- adopting techniques of experimental music such as graphic notation.

Some progressive music educators working in the 1960s and 1970s took a lead from contemporary music of the 1950s–1970s, often referred to as avant-garde music or post-war modernism. Composers of these types of music rejected conventional music and were interested in sounds and their manipulation, often using electronic means. The music education practices inspired by these contemporary musical styles represented a radical departure from traditional music education. Just as we saw with some of the early pioneers of music education, this new generation of educators railed against what they saw as wooden, narrow forms of music education based on skill training. In contrast, children's capacity to be musically creative and inventive was to be valued. They were to be given opportunities to experiment with sound and musical forms. These music educators considered there was a direct relationship between children's musical expressions and the expressions of contemporary composers. Teachers, they suggested, could focus on those relationships and thus offer children a genuine experience of music in keeping with the contemporary musical world.

Key music educators developing this approach were George Self, Brian Dennis and John Paynter. As a result of Paynter's influence and work, creative music making, composing and improvising became an established part of the English curriculum (Paynter and Aston, 1970). John Paynter and colleagues are primarily associated with music education in secondary schools. However, much of their work took place in English infant schools during the early 1960s and this work is less well known.

Principles

This return to sound and the structuring of sounds as the foundations of music found an obvious connection with young children's playful curiosity in sound. Describing his study of young children's 'playful world of sound' at the Pillsbury Foundation School in California during the period 1937–1944, Pond wrote, 'first a child becomes aware of sounds, then he or she experiences wonder and delight, and then an insatiable exploration of sound begins as wide as the environment can provide' (Pond, 1980, p. 40). He emphasised that children played with sounds, but not randomly and nor simply as a form of self-expression. According to Pond, children were interested in structuring sounds and they were inventors of sound shapes (ibid., p. 41).

The selection and organisation of sounds based on attentive, discriminatory listening was viewed as the essence of making music to many who advocated this approach to music education. This was a way, it was argued, to engage children in active self-guided music-making which also connected them to contemporary, real world music of their own time – rather than historical music of the past. Some also argued that in a contemporary world increasingly full of technological devices, teachers should help children to return to the sensory, auditory awareness of sounds *per se* and of body vibrations and to direct emotional responses to sound.

From the 1970s onwards contemporary, experimental musics have embraced a range of styles including ambient, electronic, techno, minimalism and environmental music. These musics bridged the popular and art music worlds. They share an emphasis on timbre, texture and sonic qualities to create atmosphere and mood, rather than an emphasis on melody and rhythm to create a sense of structure and direction. They often aim to impart a sense of calm and contemplation.

Listening and the Soundscape

The composer John Cage was fascinated by natural sounds in the environment. One of his most striking and radical pieces from 1952 was called '4'33''', in which the pianist sits at the piano for that length of time without playing a single note. The point of the piece was that the audience would become aware of the sounds they could hear in the concert hall during the performance. Cage wanted to challenge preconceived ideas about music and the nature of silence.

The idea of listening to the environment as music was also central to Raymond Murray Schafer's (1933–2021), ecological philosophies of sound. A Canadian composer, music educator and environmentalist, Schafer used the term *Soundscape* to describe the sonic environment, the ever-present noises with which we all live. He argued that our everyday lives have become too cluttered with noise and we need to be more aware of and aurally sensitive to acoustic environments. He was interested in the sounds of nature and listening attentively to those sounds in order to become highly attuned to their qualities.

Cage, Schafer and other artists and philosophers with similar ideas shared a sense that the soundscape is a place where the boundaries between music and nature, and nature and humanity, are blurred and where listening tunes us in to moral, spiritual, social, and environmental dimensions.

Key Text

Raymond Murray Schafer. (1994). *The Soundscape: Our sonic environment and the tuning of the world.* Rochester, VT: Destiny Books. (Originally published in 1977)

Ethnomusicologists

Ethnomusicologists, studying the music of culturally diverse social groups, have been interested in how environmental sounds have an essential role in some musical cultures. For instance, Steven Feld studied the Kaluli of Papua New Guinea and realised that acute sensitivity to the sounds of the rain forest is embedded in their culture (Feld, 2012).

Eco-literate Music Pedagogy

The term ecomusicology is used, broadly, to describe interests in music and the environment. Most recently Dan Shevock has theorised an eco-literate music pedagogy (Shevock, 2017) as a response to the climate emergency. His ideas draw on Schafer and on Satis Coleman (see p. 19) and have much in common with ecomusicology.

Eco-literate music pedagogy begins with helping children to become conscious of local places. Dan Shevock suggests that it is no small task for children today who are focused on computer and mobile phone screens to turn their attention to sounds in the environment. Because, he says, music is a way humans come to understand the world around them through sound and other senses, the sonic experiences of ecological consciousness are a fundamental aspect of eco-literate music pedagogy.

Listening and Sound as Object

Musique concrète, an experimental approach to music composition that started about 1948 in Paris, is so named because it starts from recordings of everyday sounds which already exist. Sounds are produced not only from musical instruments but from anything that will make an interesting sound. These sounds were recorded and then manipulated electronically, forming sound collages. According to Pierre Schaeffer's concept of musique concrète, sound itself can become a kind of object, detached from the source that made it.

François Delalande: Sound as Object

François Delalande had been a member of a group in France that composed musique concrète. Later he became interested in the musicality of young children aged 10–40 months attending French and Italian daycare centres (see p. 100). He combined musical concepts from musique concrète with theoretical concepts from Piaget to arrive at a distinctive approach to understanding children's early musical activity when playing certain educational percussion instruments selected by the research team. Delalande suggested that when very young children explore anything that will make a sound, they first become interested in sound objects, the single sounds alone (that is, not patterned or structured in any way).

Listening and Found Sounds

As well as listening to the soundscape and focussing on sound as object, there was a new interest among avant-garde composers in making music with novel sounds, in particular expanding the range of percussive sounds, often by incorporating everyday items or by creating new instruments. The composer John Cage composed pieces that asked for everyday items such as pots and pans, even brake drums and conch shells. The composer Harry Partch constructed unusual, novel instruments from materials such as bamboo, steel springs and gourds for performances of his composed music. The sound produced by found-sound objects is often not fixed and is indeterminate. These composers were challenging the idea that music should only be made on conventional, pitched instruments which make a pre-determined, precise sound and require specialised skills to play them.

Making music with what is available can be instant and spontaneous. Children, particularly babies and toddlers, are curious. What sound can I make with that? What sound patterns can I make? Making music with found sounds and everyday objects expands the conception of what counts as music and this expanded conception gives greater value to the playful sound-making explorations of very young children. Rather than being dismissed as merely making a noise, it is interpreted and taken seriously as musical.

Materialism

To Satis Coleman (see p. 19), working in the first decades of the twentieth century, music was more than something made by humans; music was made by all of nature (humans, non-human animals, plants and natural phenomena such as wind). Her ideas align with a recent interest in a materialist theoretical perspective. This perspective gives importance to sounds that arise not only from the actions of humans, but also from non-human sources, or 'more than human sources' as sometimes termed. Sound is dependent on all kinds of material media; the air and water that conducts the sound waves, the acoustic spaces of buildings or natural environments and living creatures that can produce all manner of sounds. So a materialist perspective suggests that all kinds of tactile, physical, material and vibrational, acoustic sensations can be part of what we consider music to be.

Image of Childhood

An open attitude to sound, being sensitive to sound and creating with sounds goes hand in hand with an open attitude towards children making music in ways that are not constrained by adult conceptions of music but accepted and valued on their own terms. Children should be given freedom to express their own voice coupled with a positive belief in children's capacity to be creative and to have something of value and originality to say.

The Approach in Practice

A book published in 1975 by Merle Chacksfield with two teacher colleagues who worked together in a large English infant school (for children aged 4–8 years), describes how they applied the creative music approach of George Self and John Paynter to their practice.

> Junk material and voice and body sounds provide a means for introducing basic musical principles. A group of children arranged a varying-sized collection of beer tins and experimented with beaters such as sticks, spoons, small metal bars and the traditional beaters, to make sounds. They discovered that the larger tins made a deeper sounds than the smaller tins, so these were then arranged in size and played again. They even discovered a simple chord of three notes, i.e. do mi so.

Later the children composed a song about the tins. This led to a discussion of rhythm and size related to sound. The work did not depend on formal musical knowledge, but the teacher introduced knowledge for the benefit of interested children. We found in our experiments in music that there is no rigid progression of work related to age for, as in all subjects, the rate of development depends on the child's ability, interest and natural talent.

(Chacksfield, Binns and Robins, 1975, p. 27)

Chacksfield and colleagues emphasised what they termed 'sound organisation'. By this term they meant listening to sounds as the fundamental material of music, exploring the possibilities of those sounds and creating with them in the same way that children might work with other artistic materials such as paint and clay. Their focus was on the developing children's ability to think in sound and on the processes of making music. It is interesting that although their approach began with creative sound experiences and graphic notation, in their book they lead quite quickly into explaining how they introduced formal musical knowledge, including staff notation and solfa.

In infant schools the provision of free play opportunities for experimentation and the flexible organisation of group work facilitated the introduction of an exploratory, creative music-making approach. Progressive approaches to music education in the first years of schooling in England had received an extra impetus after the Plowden report of 1967 which had recommended learning through discovery, drawing its rationales from Piagetian theory.

A primary reason for writing the book, these teachers explained, was that their approach was accessible to teachers who did not have formal musical skills and knowledge. In addition they described cross-curricular work, blending music with activity in other domains, language in particular, but also drama, dance and visual arts.

Their book describes the following teaching strategies.

A Focus on Listening

Attentive listening was encouraged and might be assisted by staying very still, with eyes closed. The teachers emphasised the development of aural memory for sounds. There are different types of listening.

- Embodied listening. Sounds are sensed not only in the ears and head but felt throughout the whole body as physical vibration.
- Affective listening. Sounds may evoke a particular emotion in children. For example, loud crashing sounds of a cymbal might excite or upset.
- Associative listening. Sounds may evoke associations. The associations may be connected to real-world experiences (that sounds like my

washing machine at home) or they may be imaginative (that sounds like monster footsteps).
- Objective listening. Sounds that do not evoke emotion or association are listened to, just for the objective qualities of the sound. Novel or unusual sounds will provoke this kind of listening.

The Sound Environment

The teachers focused children's attention on the soundscape, in particular the sounds of nature, or on sounds that are produced by everyday items.

Found Sounds

Chacksfield and colleagues made much use of found sounds that they referred to as junk material (beer cans, dustbin lid, pieces of heavy chain, metal mugs). They recommended that found sounds often make a better sound and are easier for children to play when suspended from a frame.

Exploring the Acoustic Properties of Instruments, Voices and Everyday Objects

Children in their school were offered space and time for experimentation with sounds so that they could make their own discoveries. The emphasis was on the processes of experimentation and problem-solving rather than arriving at some kind of finished product.

A Focus on Tone Colour and Dynamics

Attentive listening led to an appreciation of timbre, tone, dynamic and texture and differences in these qualities. The teachers pointed out that these dimensions of music often receive less attention than other dimensions such as pitch and rhythm.

Structuring with Sounds

Children's curiosity in sound and their experimentation with sounds led to the discovery of novel sonic ideas and interesting ways to combine them. The children were given opportunities to present and perform their musical discoveries and pieces for other children to listen to.

Sounds with Story

Stories lend themselves to being acted out in dramatic movement accompanied by sounds to enhance the drama of the story. These teachers also blended language activities with drama and sound.

Graphic Notation

The teachers encouraged children to use graphic notations to record their sound patterns. A graphic score uses unconventional music notation made up of signs, symbols and/or words to represent musical sounds and to indicate what a performer might play. Graphic notation was developed in the mid-twentieth century within the avant-garde movement as a way for composers to freely express musical ideas. It often includes a degree of freedom of interpretation for performers.

Graphic notation provides a valuable teaching strategy that fosters children's learning. Children are guided to interpret what they have heard, sung or played through representations that use objects or symbols (drawn or written). By translating sound into symbol, certain features of the music are fixed and highlighted. A visual (iconic) representation allows the children and educator to reflect on and discuss aspects of their music and thus develop awareness and understanding. Usefully these teachers also demonstrated how they led children into learning conventional staff notation building on their graphic notations.

Learning Progression as Horizontal

Any rigid ideas of development as fixed to age are refuted in their book. Development, these teachers argue, depends on many factors. Similarly, the progressive music educators of the late 1960s challenged the idea that learning progresses in a linear way, for example from simple to complex, as is traditionally assumed to be appropriate in the methods of music education or in cognitive explanations of learning. For these educators learning progressed in a series of events or projects that were not necessarily linked to the one that had gone before in a linear progressive way, but expanded horizontally and organically.

Comments and Connections

Approaches to nursery education – notably Froebel, Montessori and Reggio Emilia – emphasised the importance of sensory-rich material resources that stimulate exploration, imagination and play through sensory perception. Maria Montessori stressed the importance of isolating the sound properties of play objects. She had also introduced the 'game of silence'. For Montessori, active listening was not only an important basis for personal development but also provides a foundation for dialogue, cooperation and of empathy. Montessori's conception of listening as one of the basic competences for life is echoed in some of the more recent philosophies presented in this section of the book.

One risk is that approaches based on sound and listening may not challenge children sufficiently or hold high enough expectations of them.

Barbara Andress, for example, recommended the provision of opportunities for children to explore found sounds but cautioned that children should also listen to what she termed valid musical sounds. She wrote:

> they cannot grow in musical sensitivity unless provided with opportunities to hear and explore music and musical instruments that are tonally accurate and produce quality musical timbres. The child may at times play with pie tins and plastic bottles filled with rice, but must also have many experiences with fine brass cymbals and wooden maracas.
>
> (Andress et al., 1992, pp. 44–45)

Her suggestion that attention be given to the sound quality of objects or instruments aligns with the importance given to the aesthetic quality of materials by the educators of Reggio Emilia.

The primary challenge comes from those who would claim that sound exploration is not music and that sound exploration needs to progress rapidly into activities that introduce more conventional musical learning. It is interesting that in the descriptions of practice by Chacksfield and her colleagues they seem concerned to explain how the children's creative activities could lead quite rapidly into opportunities to introduce formal skills and knowledge such as solfa and notation. It is as if they recognised the gap between the learning children acquire from their self-guided explorations and the content of a formal curriculum, and sought ways to bridge that gap. Others would argue that exploratory and open-ended approaches allow children to develop musical ideas that are in keeping with their own imaginative directions, whatever those might be. It is the responsibility of the adult to try to understand and enter the child's musical world, on the assumption that it is musical, and to identify the learning content. This is when observation and careful listening, as with the pedagogy of Reggio Emilia for example, enables the teacher to identify the musical thinking and intentions behind what may at first appear to be random explorations of sounds.

Nevertheless as children's work with explorations of sounds continues, how to extend and develop it can be a challenge for educators. This raises the long-standing dilemma for teachers between allowing children the freedom to experiment with musical ideas and develop their musical thinking and creativity, balanced against the need for structured teaching of music-specific concepts and techniques. Interestingly, critics of the creative music movement, particularly during its heyday in the 1970s and 1980s, argued that it could become just as one-sided and dogmatic as more formal, teacher-led approaches. They suggested that a well-rounded music education would include a combination of child-centred, creative, exploratory activity balanced by formal instruction.

Bibliography

Andress, L. B., Heimann, H., Rinehart, C. and Talbert, G. (1992). Music in early childhood: The environment. In B. L. Andress and L. Miller Walker (eds), *Readings in Early Childhood Music Education*. Reston, VA: Music Educators National Conference.

Chacksfield, K. M., Binns, P. A. and Robins, V. M. (1975). *Music and Language with Young Children*. Oxford: Basil Blackwell.

Feld, S. (2012). *Sound and Sentiment: Birds, weeping, poetics, and song in Kaluli expression, 3rd Edition*. Durham, NC: Duke University Press.

Paynter, J. and Aston, P. (1970). *Sound and Silence: Classroom projects in creative music*. Cambridge: Cambridge University Press.

Pond, D, (1980). The young child's playful world of sound. *Music Educators Journal*, 66(7), 38–41.

Schafer, R. M. (1994). *The Soundscape: Our sonic environment and the tuning of the world*. Rochester, VT: Destiny Books. (Originally published in 1977)

Shevock, D. (2017). *Eco-Literate Music Pedagogy*. London: Taylor and Francis.

15 Communicative Musicality

> Music is at the centre of what it means to be human – it is the sounds of human bodies and minds moving in creative, story-making ways.
> (Malloch and Trevarthen, 2018)

During the 1970s researchers became interested in studying babies and how they interacted with others. What they found started to challenge the view, held widely until then, that babies were passive and merely responding to the world around them. On the contrary, these researchers showed that babies are active, sociable and have competences that enable them to communicate.

One of these researchers, Colwyn Trevarthen, analysed interactions between mothers and their babies and was able to show that even a newborn has the ability to initiate a two-way communication. He proposed that the motivation to be sociable is inborn and showed how babies communicate through eye contact, facial expressions and small gestures. In the late 1990s, collaborating with the musician Stephen Malloch, the two of them became very interested in the musical characteristics of adult-infant interaction and together they extended these ideas into a theory Stephen Malloch termed 'communicative musicality' (Malloch and Trevarthen, 1999). This theory proposes that all communication is based on innate human capacities that are, at core, musical in character and that music has a communicative purpose.

Trevarthen did not evolve a pedagogical approach for music education. However he is an enthusiastic and generous disseminator of his theoretical ideas and they have become widely known. Since the late 1990s the provision of baby and toddler music classes has expanded rapidly and the discoveries of music-like processes driving early communication have inspired pedagogical approaches, particularly with under-3-year-olds. His explanation of infant competences has provided important validations for musical activity with babies and toddlers.

Theories of adult-infant interaction have:

- expanded our knowledge base of development from birth to 3 years
- emphasised the centrality of emotional-social development

- identified the processes of adult-infant interaction and their musical features, and
- provided models for how adults may interact and play with young children to support musical learning.

Colwyn Trevarthen (1931 –)

Colwyn Trevarthen originally studied biology in New Zealand and in 1966 went to Harvard University to join the Center for Cognitive Studies where he was involved in research in infant communication alongside Jerome Bruner. He then joined the University of Edinburgh in 1971 and had a long career of research and teaching at the university as Professor of Child Psychology and Psychobiology.

Communicative Musicality: The Theory

Since 2000 the theory of communicative musicality has made a major contribution to the field of music psychology and been an important influence on early childhood music education pedagogy. However, the origins of this theory go back to the late 1970s when the field of infant communication studies started to use microanalysis of video recordings as a method. Microanalysis involved frame by frame replay of short clips of video, usually extracted from longer sequences of interaction between a mother and her baby. This detailed analysis of slow playback video revealed finer details of interaction that were not obvious from real time observation.

In 1979 Colwyn Trevarthen isolated the sound track from video recordings of mother-baby interactions and subjected them to acoustic analysis. The babies, awake, calm and alert, were reclining in a baby chair with the mothers facing them. The analyses showed how mothers would typically join in with imitative sounds that invited the babies' coos and other small sounds and gave them meaning to create a kind of shared conversation. Years later, in 1996, Stephen Malloch, at Edinburgh University, listened to these tapes of mothers and their babies 'chatting' with each other.

> As I listened, intrigued by the fluid give and take of the communication, and the lilting speech of the mother as she chatted with her baby, I began to tap my foot. I am, by training, a musician, so I was very used to automatically feeling the beat as I listened to musical sounds … I replaced the tape, and again, I could sense a distinct rhythmicity and melodious give and take to the gentle prompting of Laura's mother and the pitched vocal replies from Laura …. A few weeks later, as I walked down the stairs to Colwyn's main lab, the words 'communicative musicality' came into my mind as a way of describing what I had heard.
>
> (Malloch and Trevarthen, 2018, pp. 3–4)

Stephen Malloch had found regular patterns of timing in the exchanges between the mother and her baby and so he proposed that infant communication is intrinsically musical. Further work followed using spectrographs and plotting the pitch of the interactions between the mother and baby pairs so that this theory of communicative musicality could be based on more precise identification of the parameters of pulse, tone quality and narrative (Malloch and Trevarthen, 1999).

Malloch and Trevarthen went on to propose that this musical communication is conveyed multi-modally, via gesture, gaze, and vocalisations, between mother and baby. They suggested that it reflects innate abilities and motivations to connect emotionally via these modes of communication. The mother is attuned to the baby's state of arousal and attention and modifies her vocalisations and gestures in response.

Communicative musicality joins other work in a similar vein. Research from a number of sources had contributed to the idea that parents and baby are involved in communication with musical qualities. Hanuš and Metcheld Papoušek reflected on their interactions with their own baby (Papoušek and Papoušek, 1981) and suggested that parents intuitively modify their infant-directed speech to be emotionally communicative. They suggested that infant-directed speech includes smooth, bell-shaped pitch contours, one-syllable utterances and prolonged vowel sounds. They were perhaps the first to highlight the musical character of these adult-infant exchanges. They suggested that parents vary these vocalisations to create a playful build-up of arousal followed by release. Playing peepo with a baby is a good example of this build-up and release pattern.

Daniel Stern proposed the idea of 'vitality forms' to capture how the human mind encodes dynamic experiences (Stern, 1998). These he suggests are crucial for interpersonal interactions and performance arts such as dance and music. He described social play between adult and baby as a context in which the adult, using all modes, playfully manipulates the vitality forms. Baby rhymes and singing games are rich with vitality forms.

Similarly Ellen Dissanayake (2000) has suggested that narrative structures made up of vocalisations (speech and singing), gestures and facial expressions, that are seen as babies interact with loving caregivers are the universal fundamentals of what becomes music, dance and theatre.

It is a small step from these theoretical ideas for music educators to suggest that innate communicative musicality can be encouraged and strengthened through sensitive, playful interactions with babies and toddlers and that these exchanges are foundational to learning. What's more, these interactions are a way for infant and parent to express and share emotional states with one another, and so they also contribute to the development of positive adult-infant relationships.

Key Text

Sandra Smidt. (2017). *Introducing Trevarthen: A guide for practitioners and students in early years education.* London: Routledge.

Principles

Infant-Directed Speech

In the 1970s the field of research into early communication patterns between mothers and their babies living in westernised countries revealed that babies respond enthusiastically to a version of talk that is:

- at a higher pitch and with more rise and fall of pitch than in normal adult speech
- at a slower pace, with short phrases and pauses between phrases, and
- full of simple repetitions of the short phrases and with a circling quality, such as, 'hello baby', 'hello baby', 'oh, are you hungry', 'are you hungry then?'.

Initially this type of talk was called 'motherese' but now it is more usually termed 'infant-directed speech' because anyone, mothers, fathers, older siblings or other adult carers, will modify their speech in this way. Infant directed speech also encourages close contact and mutual gazing between the adults and babies. Importantly, infant-directed speech involves more than just vocal production. It contains emotional communicative messages conveyed through a combination of pitch, touch, facial expressions, gestures and vocal tone. Many purposes have been proposed for infant-directed speech including gaining baby's attention, communicating emotion and closeness and supporting language learning.

Infant-Directed Singing

From about 3 months of age in many (probably all) cultures, mothers start to sing baby songs to their infants. These are the characteristics of baby songs (Malloch and Trevarthen, 2018).

- The beat is clear and precise; usually at a slow to moderate pace.
- The beat is often marked by regular movements of the baby's body, or by small claps or taps.
- The singer adopts a clear vocal tone, in a light, higher pitch, and marked rise and fall phrasing to develop the emotional narrative of the song.
- The songs have a simple structure, usually four lines each of around three or four beats.
- There may be musical 'tricks' such as slowing down or making a sudden accent, to vary the beat and to mark a climax and resolution.

Image of Babyhood

Communicative musicality incorporates a strong image of the baby as competent from birth, as sociable and agentic. This image of the competent infant represented a radical change from the prior image of babies as passive and incompetent.

This image is, however, based on a westernised and contemporary conception of babyhood in which families are typically small and mothers are expected to devote time and effort not only to the physical care of their babies but also to their intellectual and sociable development. Some have criticised this image from two perspectives, 1) because it tends towards an unrealistically idealised image of babyhood and 2) because it represents a construction of babyhood that is dominant in middle class, white, westernised families. In relation to the world's total population this social group represents only a small minority of families and babies.

The Theory in Practice

This example activity is taken from an observation of a baby music session:

> A circle of 8 mothers and one father with 6-month and older babies who attend a weekly baby music group are sitting on cushions with their babies in front of them, most of them propped up on more cushions. Parent and baby face one another. They are playing 'beepo' using chiffon scarves. The parents sing a short song, taught to them a week ago, which ends by pulling away the scarf. The song arrives at a climax, 'beepo!'. Rosie, the music educator, encourages the parents to sing individually and responsively with their baby, reading their babies' cues, and leaves them to play the game in their own time, rather than lead the group in unison.
>
> One baby has lost interest in the song and beepo activity and has become focused on scrunching the scarf with both hands and making expressive noises to match her actions. Rosie notices this. She copies the movement and the noises. The baby stops for a moment, looks at her, smiles, and repeats her scrunchy action and noise. Rosie repeats. After a couple of repetitions Rosie exaggerates the action and noise, making it more energetic and louder. The baby squeals with excitement and copies. After a couple more turns, baby is squealing more and more, so Rosie decides it is time to 'wind down' the game, with a much quieter, slower turn.

The educator:

- introduces a rhyme and game that will engender interactive play and encourages the parents to play responsively
- allows each parent and baby pair to play the song-game individually, rather than in unison as a whole group, so that each pair can attune and play in their own way
- is alert to what the babies are doing

- copies what one child does as exactly as possible, matching gesture, vocalisation, dynamic quality and pace
- sustains a copying game with repetitions
- varies the repetitions a little, enough to maintain but not lose interest
- regulates the emotional dynamic of the game with enough stimulation to maintain interest and involvement, but not too much, and
- assists the child in 'winding down'.

The expression 'parents are children's first educators' is now familiar. How parents can be more directly participative in the music session is informed by the theory of communicative musicality. Rosie had taught the 'beepo' baby song with the scarves the previous week and then initiated it the following week, leaving the parents to play it independently, rather than conform to a whole group activity. She observed carefully, however. Her aim was to:

- develop methods of working with parents that are respectful and inclusive
- develop approaches that built on what parents do already and are meaningful to them, and
- encourage parents to interact responsively with their babies.

The theory has influenced some projects that have worked in daycare settings with the staff, encouraging them to use more singing in their care for babies, to understand its contribution and to appreciate the value of doing so. The Babysong project described in the Froebel section (see p. 33) is a leading example.

The concept of communicative musicality includes the key idea that infants and caregivers can attune to one another's emotional states and that singing can be a conduit for emotional exchange to the benefit of both. It can support the mother's feelings of wellbeing and sense of being connected to her baby. Some baby and mother music work emphasises these mutual gains and may, in addition, support mothers in their recovery from postnatal depression (Fancourt and Perkins, 2017).

Comments and Connections

Colwyn Trevarthen's early work with Bruner means that there are connections between his work and those of Bruner, especially in relation to ideas of narrative and babies' motivations to become participating members of their own culture. In addition to similarities with Bruner's work, it is important to acknowledge the other researchers who made contributions to this field of early infant communication and its musical qualities.

Although communicative musicality is an influential theory at the present time, it is not without criticism. Some suggest that these theoretical ideas emphasise the mother and baby relationship above all others. This emphasis is criticised both from a feminist perspective and from a research method perspective. Researchers have shown that babies are equally interested in and readily interact with other babies, their siblings and adults who are not their primary caregiver.

The idea that babies are sociable and agentic brought about an important shift in thinking from the earlier conception of babies as passive. However, some argue that to hold an image of young babies as special, sociable and clever is very appealing to westernised adults. As a result more is being imputed in babies' actions than is actually happening and adults – whether researchers, parents or educators – are viewing through rose-tinted spectacles.

Moreover the proposal that infant-directed speech is a universal practice is contested. Anthropologists have found many cultures where infant-directed speech is not practised in the way that is generally found among westernised parents and carers. They argue that culturally specific beliefs and practices shape the interactions of adults with babies in their communities and there is no single universal model for nurturing babies (DeLoache and Gottlieb, 2000). In cultures, for example, where babies are carried in slings almost constantly (by the mother or other carers), breast fed on demand and sleep with their mothers, they may rely more on bodily contact and movement as a form of communication to create responsiveness and closeness. Therefore the idea that babies are socially capable and able to communicate reflects an image of babies that is not found worldwide and may reflect cultural beliefs rather than truths.

Following a similar line of argument, singing to babies, some argue, is multi-cultural but not universal. It presumes a particular representation of good parenting and carer behaviour that is embedded in western parenting culture. This cultural conception of good parenting contains assumptions that need to be engaged with reflectively and critically rather than accepted as the norm. It assumes that mothers have time to devote to their babies and that they think that playing with babies is important. In an informative book, anthropologist David Lancy (2017) suggests that certain ideas about babyhood and childhood that are thought to be essential and universal, are in fact defined by affluent westernised parents living in specific circumstances.

Bibliography

DeLoache, J.S. and Gottlieb, A. (2000). *A World of Babies: Imagined childcare guides for seven societies*. Cambridge: Cambridge University Press.

Dissanayake, E. (2000). *Art and Intimacy: How the arts began*. Seattle, WA: University of Washington Press.

Fancourt, D. and Perkins, R. (2017). Associations between singing to babies and symptoms of postnatal depression, wellbeing, self-esteem and mother–infant bond. *Public Health*, 145, 149–152.

Lancy, D. (2017). *Raising Children: Surprising insights from other cultures*. Cambridge: Cambridge University Press.

Malloch, S. and Travarthen, C. (1999). Mothers and infants and communicative musicality. *Musicae Scientiae*, 3(1), 29–57.

Malloch, S. and Trevarthen, C. (2009). Musicality: Communicating the vitality and interests of life. In S. Malloch and C. Trevarthen (eds.), *Communicative Musicality: Exploring the basis of human companionship*, pp. 1–11. Oxford: Oxford University Press.

Malloch, S. and Trevarthen, C. (2018). The human nature of music. *Frontiers in Psychology*, 9, 1680.

Papousek, M. and Papoušek, H. (1981). Musical elements in the infant's vocalization: Their significance for communication, cognition, and creativity. *Advances in Infancy Research*, 1, 163–224.

Stern, D. N. (1998). *The Interpersonal World of the Infant: A view from psychoanalysis and developmental psychology*. London: Karnac Books.

16 Music Play and Playful Pedagogies

> The life of the young child is free, fluid and dynamic – a series of seemingly unrelated episodes. His kaleidoscopic transitions often include the conscious and unconscious production of sounds. He intones and sings quietly to himself as he plays by himself or in the company of others; he imitates the sounds he hears; he experiments with his physical movements and hears the rhythmic patterns sounded by his feet, etc. Sounds, patterns, and organizational schemes, therefore, are not separate from the child's world of play. There is no sharp division in the child's mind between musical and non-musical experience. For the child, then, a musical experience is not an isolated thing, but is interrelated with his whole living experience.
>
> (Biasini, Thomas and Pogonowski, 1971)

As the quote above suggests, musical play is blended into children's 'ways of being' in the world, so that it is almost impossible to separate out the musical from general play. Early childhood education has a strong tradition of valuing children's play and for developing pedagogies which support children's learning in and through play. The value of play was endorsed by educational philosophers and theorists as long ago as Froebel and has been incorporated into the pedagogies of many theorists and philosophers included in this book. They, in turn, have provided inspiration for music pedagogies that foster children's learning through musical play.

Historically, evolving philosophies and theories of children's learning in music have given rise to varying conceptions of musical play. These conceptions, in turn, suggest varying rationales in support of the value of musical play in education and suggest different pedagogical approaches that might connect with and extend children's musical play. Philosophies associated with progressive ideas of education respect children's own creativity and imagination and suggest that children should have the freedom to explore their own interests, at their own pace. Progressive educators argue that, through play, children can become independent and imaginative musical thinkers. In contrast, pedagogies and practices associated with more traditional conceptions of education might value playful activities but as a medium for learning skills and knowledge determined in advance by the teacher. Whether the adult or the child initiates play, whether the child is left free to develop their play in their own directions, or the adult joins in, and guides the direction of play – these are all important questions to be considered.

In the 1990s and at the turn of the twenty-first century there were two developments that gave a particular impetus to creative and play pedagogies in music education. First there was an increasing interest in children's own, self-initiated music-making and musical cultures. Second policies and practices to promote creativity became prominent and there was a strong turn to creative teaching and learning. In the UK, however, this period has been relatively short-lived, and in more recent years it has been replaced by an emphasis on core skills of literacy and numeracy and pressure to prepare pre-school children for the demands of formal, adult-directed learning in mainstream schooling.

Children's Music and Musical Cultures

The music that children make up themselves, spontaneous and improvised, has captured the interest of educators and researchers stretching back to the early years of the twentieth century. In the 1930s Donald Pond spent several years documenting the music-making of young children who attended a nursery in California (Pond, 1980). This nursery had been equipped with instruments and other resources designed to encourage music play. His descriptions remain an important source of information about the music children make when left to their own devices. A range of research studies in subsequent years added to and confirmed Pond's conclusions that young children have the ability to generate music that, rather than being random and disorganised (as is often assumed), has intention, structure, meaning and artistry (Marsh and Young, 2006).

In the 1990s and onwards sociologists and ethnomusicologists became interested in children's everyday lives and their musical cultures. Patricia Shehan Campbell is both an educator and ethnomusicologist and she observed children attending a pre-school throughout their day (Campbell, 2010). She described their spontaneous musical expressions and how these formed a constant sound track to the children's lives. She proposed that children used music for self-expression, to interact with others and to entertain themselves. Interest in children's musical worlds has continued to grow with researchers studying children's music in different cultural contexts and tracking how children's musical worlds have changed with the increasing presence of music technology (Marsh, 2008).

The interest in children's music and musical cultures raised important questions for educators. Is this a separate strand of activity that children are in complete control of, that takes place outside of education music sessions and should remain so? Pond, for example, advocated leaving children to play musically in their own ways and not to interfere. Or is it a range of musical activities that should be connected with, built on and incorporated into music education both because it is important to children's musical identities and because it forms an important resource for learning? In my own work, I have suggested ways of playing musically with young children in order to extend their musical learning (Young, 2003).

Key Text

Patricia Shehan Campbell. (2010). *Songs in their Heads: Music and its meaning in children's lives*, 2nd edition. Oxford: Oxford University Press.

Philosophies and Theories of Musical Play

For Froebel, young children's play was not trivial but serious, and he promoted the idea that play should be nurtured through the provision of appropriate resources and through adult guidance. The importance of providing resources that encourage different types of play is embedded in early childhood practice and nurseries and pre-schools will typically provide sound makers and instruments suitable for young children in order to foster free musical play. Babies might be provided with treasure baskets filled with everyday small items that make interesting sounds.

Donald Pond's work in the special music nursery during the late 1930s was part of the child study movement that was dominant in the USA at that time. He believed that children possessed an innate 'natural musicality' which they would reveal if they were free to play in an environment equipped with inviting instruments and offering space for moving and dancing. He interpreted children's musical play through a reconceptualist lens, making links between the rhythmic activity and improvised singing of children and early musical forms (Pond, 1980). He thought it essential that educators not stifle children's own music-making, and that if children were provided with genuinely interesting instruments and given time, space and opportunity to make their own music, then they would discover for themselves much about how to pattern sounds, combine them and sequence them into meaningful musical forms. His pedagogical recommendations focussed on providing an environment for musical play and being an interested listener, rather than intervening in any way.

The psychoanalytic pedagogy of Susan Isaacs suggested to Eunice Bailey that musical play is important to a child's emotional development (see p. 55). It is, she proposed, a means for children to express themselves and release subconscious feelings, including negative feelings, thus resolving inner conflict and growing in self-discipline and cooperation with other children. She therefore provided opportunities for children to engage in fantasy (*sic*.) play that included music, drama and dance. These expressive, make-believe forms of play were the means, she thought, through which children made discoveries in music. Orff educators also value make-believe and narrative play in which music is interwoven with dance, drama and poetry and Orff considered children's own cultural play forms to be the setting-off point for music education. Orff pedagogy, however, provides children with the building blocks for improvisation; the adult is the initiator rather than the child.

These historical play theories have both strengths and weaknesses. The weaknesses may arise from beliefs about subconscious emotional energy or about evolution and 'primitivism' that we would now consider outdated. The strengths lie in their convictions of the value of musical play, different types of environment to promote musical play and their descriptions of its musical detail. These ideas about musical play are valuable to know about and consider because they have provided a foundation for more recent play theories.

The influence of Piagetian theory and later Vygotskian theory focused interest onto the relationship between play and young children's cognitive development. From their constructivist views of learning, both sought to explain how children construct concepts, knowledge and skills through play. They suggested that in play children are able to set their own goals and challenges defined by their own cognitive drives and current capabilities. While the role of play as a shaping force in the development of children's thought and action has been recognised for some time, the musical dimensions of children's play have been less well understood. Danette Littleton, starting from a strong belief in the naturalness of musical play, called upon Piagetian theory to explain musical play within the context of children's cognitive development, delineating practice play, symbolic play and games with rules (Littleton, 1998).

Some theorists explain a direct relationship between play process *per se* and cognitive development while others suggest that adults or other children foster children's learning in play through forms of support and input. Certainly the sociocultural turn in the 1990s offered an important new lens through which to view children's musical play. Researchers viewing children's musical play through sociocultural lens demonstrated the ways in which children exercise cultural agency in the self-initiated musical play that occurs in the informal spaces and places of schools and communities. Amanda Niland (2009) observed children playing musically and adopted sociocultural theory, mainly from Vygotsky, to interpret their sociable musical play, peers playing with peers, and also to explain how she herself, as a teacher, connected with their playful activity to extend and develop it. In my own work I developed a way of playing interactively with children when they were playing instruments that adopted the turn-taking of adult-infant interaction, drawing also on theories of communicative musicality (Young, 2003).

Increasing concern for sensitivity to children's home backgrounds and cultural identity led to analyses of children's musical play which revealed connections with their wider family, social and cultural lives. Claudia

Gluschankof, for example, identified differences in the musical play of Israeli Arab and Israeli Jewish children attending the same setting that reflected their home musical backgrounds (Gluschankof, 2008).

Danette Littleton

Danette Littleton (1998) observed musical play in educational settings and, by drawing on various theoretical ideas, identified different styles of musical play. These include:

- co-operative music play: children participate in sociable, interactive musical activity
- functional music play: children are exploring the sound-making potential of a range of materials and experimenting with techniques
- constructive musical play: functional music play extends into creative improvisation and composition
- dramatic musical play: children integrate music making with dramatic and role play
- kinaesthetic music play: children focus on movement or dance as a playful response to music
- games with rules: children engage in group-oriented, structured musical games such as singing games or clapping games.

Littleton explained that the role of the teacher is to make provision for the different types of musical play.

Key Text

Danette Littleton. (2015). *When Music Goes to School: Perspectives on learning and teaching.* Lanham, MD: Rowman & Littlefield.

Singing Games

Singing games are often included in discussions of musical play but have very specific characteristics. Singing games are ready-made, part of a tradition and are, traditionally, handed on between children. While they may well be creatively modified by children, they are nevertheless based on a premade cultural format. They are sociable play, played between two children or groups of children and the participating children conform to the patterned movements and song structures. Teachers introduce singing games to children with a number of combined learning aims. They will aim for the children to:

- learn a repertoire of rhymes, songs and movement play that belong to certain musical traditions
- gain experience of learning to sing and to coordinate their movements in time with the music, and with others in their group

162 Part V

- gain direct experience of musical elements, such as structure, rhythm, melody, and
- experience the pleasure of participating, collectively in games and the intrinsic motivation of sociable play.

Image of Childhood

The image of childhood behind ideas of music play broadly emphasises the child as possessing an innate musicality and being able to use that musicality for self-expression, for connection in sociable activity with others and for self-guided learning. Children are viewed as active and competent participants in the learning process. Progressive and play-based approaches may lean towards a romantic view of childhood, based on freedom, innocence and child-like ways of being.

The Theories in Practice

> *Five 3-year-olds in an early childhood centre are playing outside on the outdoor equipment. One of them reaches the top of a small slide and in a sing-song voice calls out, 'I'm on the slide, I'm on the slide'. The adult who is watching the slide, hears the child and responds to her, 'you're on the slide, you're on the slide' in a matching vocal style. The child hears her, turns and they smile briefly at one another. The child whizzes down the slide and runs off.*

This small example illustrates how for young children song and speech are often neither one nor the other, but contain elements of both. It also illustrates how children integrate vocal play into other forms of ongoing activity, so that it is woven into multi-modal play. One element is inseparable from the others. The singing play is embedded in the activity of playing on the slide. This small example also illustrates a key characteristic of music play and playful pedagogy, that it often takes place in fleeting moments. The educator is listening and alert and responds, in the moment, to the child's singing.

The aim of music play pedagogy is to build on children's play interests and the musical (and language) thinking they reveal as they play. In this way teachers can promote learning aims while still maintaining the essential characteristics of play. This is why teachers need both music knowledge and pedagogical knowledge as well as confidence, initiative and a playful attitude, to capture the learning moment.

> *A 4-year-old sits behind an Orff xylophone which is set on the floor, holding two felt beaters. A nursery practitioner joins him, sitting opposite, also holding two beaters. She looks at him and waits. He plays a single note, very deliberately and then looks up at her. She copies that strike exactly. He strikes another and again looks at her in anticipation. She copies. He*

then rubs the beater slowly up and down the keys, making a quiet sound. Again, the practitioner copies his action. He plays a small rhythmic phrase on several different notes and looks up. The practitioner plays it back to him. He plays exactly the same phrase again. The exchange continues in this musical dialogue for a few more turns until they are interrupted by another child and the exchange stops, quite suddenly.

In this play episode, the adult waits and when the child looks up, interprets that as an invitation to join in. She joins in by copying and creating a musical dialogue.

Creating the Environment

Space

The adults provide suitable spaces for music play that are attractive and inviting. Ideally the space is large enough and uncluttered to allow for free movement activity. Ideally too the space will accommodate the sound of music play within the setting as a whole. In fine weather a music play area can be set up outside.

Resources

The teacher provides the resources for music play and these may include sounding materials of various kinds; pitched, non-pitched, and electronic instruments; equipment that will play recorded music, audio and video recorders; print resources such as pictures, picture books and songbooks; drama and movement resources such as costumes, puppets, pieces of fabric, scarves or ribbons; and a range of teacher-prepared resources such as game boards, flash cards, or listening guides. It is important to ring the changes with the music play resources. One week the music resources may consist of baskets with variety of wooden instruments, another week a music line outside with metal sounding objects strung from it and another week perhaps a single, large djembe is set out.

Structures and Stimuli

The adult may decide to introduce a certain stimulus, sometimes called a 'provocation', or to introduce certain structures that will support and generate the children's playfulness and creativity. The presence of an adult willing to play also constitutes a form of structure.

Access

The adult decides how the children are to be invited to the music play area – perhaps they can access it as part of free play, or they are invited in small groups, or even wait their turn in pairs or individually.

In all these aspects of provision the adult is subtly initiating the play; by providing, inviting, even perhaps modelling and demonstrating. But as much as possible the initiative is handed back to the child and there is no fixed, framework or pre-determined goal to the play.

Observing and Listening Musically

The adult observes and listens. When children are aware that the adult listens to them attentively it has a positive effect on children's play. Typically their play becomes more focused and prolonged. The adult adopts a listening approach that assumes the children's play has intention and is musical. When it is received and heard as music, it becomes musical. This strategy is in keeping with Dewey who proposed that we should not ask 'what is music' but 'when' is music (see p. 40).

Scaffolding, Modelling and Responding

When the educator listens attentively, they start to notice the detail of children's musical play. Without this conscious awareness, learning and teaching opportunities may be overlooked or misinterpreted. There is then a careful judgement to be made about how to act next. The challenge is to wait, think and not rush to intervene. Some children will offer an invitation, others may not. Teachers are often over-keen to direct, explain, demonstrate or ask questions.

Joining in with Play

Adults may join in with musical play, but importantly will do so on the children's terms and not seek to control or limit the child's musical playfulness. They may respond by copying. They vocalise, sing, move or play an exact copy of something that the child has done. This simple act of imitating both validates what the child has done and provides an opportunity for them to hear back their own musical production.

The adult may respond by offering something that matches, but is not exactly the same. In this kind of response the adult offers an extension or a challenge. Alternatively the adult may join in with singing, playing or moving, at the same time as the child. In this kind of synchronised play, the adult joins in with matching musical play that creates a duet. Again, this must be carefully judged so that it doesn't overwhelm or close down the child's play, but adds to it and extends it.

Talking

Quite likely the music play contributions by the adult take place without talk, only musical communication, especially with babies and toddlers.

Stopping the flow of music play to ask a question or emphasise some aspect of musical learning can be counter-productive in terms of children's learning and the musicality of the moment. However, there can be a place for advice, instruction or prompting with older children. Commenting and describing is a valuable strategy for drawing children's attention to musical aspects and developing their understanding perhaps by starting to name musical elements. Asking open questions can be an important aspect of scaffolding children's musical play. Open questions also encourage problem-solving that stimulates musical thinking. In these kinds of questions the adult does not have a fixed answer in mind, but asks questions to suggest, or extend children's musical play. 'I wonder what would happen if ...'?

Comments and Connections

Playful music pedagogy is rarely integrated either within general practice in early childhood settings or within the more music-centred models of practice offered by specialist music educators. Given the emphasis on the value of play to children's learning and the emphasis on constructivist-based learning, this is surprising. Play pedagogy in music education is overshadowed by a strong tradition of teacher-led, didactic learning. So much so that some music educators can feel redundant when they are not leading music learning experiences. Equally teachers may have concerns about the possible noise and classroom management challenges that may arise in music play activities. There is the additional difficulty that educators are often tied to the expectations of parents, managers and headteachers who have purchased or commissioned their services and who expect a formal, product-focused approach over process, self-guided learning approaches.

Adult-led forms of music pedagogy may seem to promote achievement in certain skill areas and knowledge and to do so quite efficiently. However, learning through approaches in which children are taking the initiative and making self-motivated choices can lead to more secure and deeper conceptual learning and also support the development of independent and imaginative musical thinking. Through play children have the opportunity to actively drive their own musical learning and development. They can use play to adapt socially and culturally. For example, they may learn to accommodate to playing with other children or they may learn to connect the music they know from their home lives to music they encounter in the setting. It is also important to recognise that play is not a one-off event but linked and accumulative over time. Children typically revisit play ideas they find rewarding and interesting, and rework and extend them.

As a result of the dominance of teacher-led approaches to music pedagogy, how children play musically and learn through musical play are not always appreciated and understood. So music play pedagogy is less well developed than other pedagogical approaches in early childhood practice. It can easily be reduced to a few, superficial, free-play activities or replaced by adult-structured tasks disguised as 'playful learning'. Teachers may be concerned that children do not seem to be learning anything of value from play. It is important to stress that it is not about leaving the children to play on their own, without intervention. It can be useful to think of teacher involvement on a continuum from, at one end providing and standing back through all levels of participation to, at the other end, full participation in joint play.

The question that musical play always raises is the extent to which children can learn the important aspects of musical skill and knowledge that they might be expected to learn in a music education through their own self-motivated play. There have been several points in this book where this gap between self-motivated learning and learning the conventional skills and knowledge of music has been discussed. For example, Frances Aronoff's wordy descriptions of music teaching interactions (see p. 124) seek to capture the interactions between children and adults in which the adult is bridging the gap between the children's interests and their self-generated actions and the curriculum content to be learnt.

It is also important not to view through rose-tinted lens and consider that unfettered musical play is always a good thing. Play may become repetitive and get stuck at a low-level or it may reproduce stereotypes of race or gender and should be challenged. Some neuro-diverse children may be upset by the exuberant playful activity of other children, particularly if they are creating a lot of noise. Sometimes adult intervention to stop and re-direct may be necessary.

The arrival of rapidly evolving digital media complicate the way children play with music and we need new ways of observing, understanding and theorising musical play. These revised understandings of musical play will then suggest new pedagogical practices. As yet, there is very little work in this area.

Bibliography

Biasini, A., Thomas, R. B. and Pogonowski, L. (1971). Manhattanville Music Curriculum Program: Interaction. Retrieved from https://files.eric.ed.gov/fulltext/ED045865.pdf.

Campbell, P. S. (2010). *Songs in their Heads: Music and its meaning in children's lives*, 2nd edition. Oxford: Oxford University Press.

Gluschankof, C. (2008). Musical expressions in kindergarten: An inter-cultural study? *Contemporary Issues in Early Childhood*, 9(4), 317–327.

Littleton, D. (1998). Music learning and child's play. *General Music Today*, 12(1), 8–15.

Marsh, K. (2008). *The Musical Playground: Global tradition and change in children's songs and games*. Oxford: Oxford University Press.

Marsh, K. and Young, S. (2006). Musical play. In G. McPherson (ed.), *The Child as Musician: A handbook of musical development*, pp. 289–310. Oxford: Oxford University Press.

Niland, A. (2009). The power of musical play: The value of play-based, child-centered curriculum in early childhood music education. *General Music Today*, 23(1), 17–21.

Pond, D. (1980). The young child's playful world of sound. *Music Educators Journal*, 66(7), 38–41.

Young, S. (2003). *Music with the Under-Fours*. London: Routledge.

17 Addressing Diversity

> Do things fall apart, or prove ineffective, when they do not reflect demographic change, do not respond to cultural variation and do not reasonably reform to meet the needs of a new era? Can music education remain relevant and useful through the full-scale continuation of conventional practices, or is there something prophetic in the statement that things fall apart in music education, if there are insufficient efforts to revise and adapt to societal evolution?
>
> (Campbell, 2018, p. ix)

Music represents and identifies people, cultures and communities. Therefore it is never 'purely music', it always carries wider connotations. Social and cultural considerations should thus play a part in decisions about content and pedagogical approach in music education. Looking back at the methods and approaches presented in this book, it becomes clear that their content and pedagogy have been dominated by European music traditions. As Patricia Shehan Campbell writes, in the quote above, 'can music education remain relevant and useful … if there are insufficient efforts to revise and adapt to societal evolution?'

Philosophies of education that we read about earlier in the book often contained ideals for transforming society for the better through education. The educators of Reggio Emilia aim to foster a democratic society and Montessori wished for a harmonious society living in peace, to give but two examples tied to particular times and places. Music education, therefore, has a responsibility to be alert to current social contexts and how education can promote positive social change. Inequalities, as a consequence of race, gender, religion and physical ability represent a social issue that education can address.

From Songs of 'Other Lands' to Decolonising

Until the 1970s music education for young children was based on European or North American children's folk songs and European art music. Occasionally song collections might include songs from 'other lands'; notated even if the original had never been notated and with lyrics always in English, translated if necessary. The aim was a simple one, to add some colour and variation to the repertoire. Songs were selected because they were musically suitable for children's voices and represented some kind of learning purpose within westernised music practices. Little thought was given to the original meanings of the song to the people who first owned it, their musical traditions, performance styles or the ways in which the song was traditionally taught and learned.

From the 1980s onwards the curriculum expanded to include more diverse musics. However the reason for this expansion derived more from the changing demographic of children being taught than a philosophy and purpose of music education. The aim was to make immigrant cultures more visible and valued, to celebrate cultural difference while seeking to diminish any forms of discrimination. In the UK, the content might include music from the Caribbean and South Asia, reflecting the immigrant populations of urban cities. The cultural breadth rarely expanded beyond these styles and genres of music.

Around the same time, ethnomusicology departments in universities expanded to teach musics from (among other places) India, Indonesia and the African continent. Publications for music education followed suit providing recordings, information, songs and activities for classroom instruments. The emphasis was on repertoire, information and activities rather than cultural meaning or teaching the music via pedagogical approaches that would be true to that musical style.

However, I should add that few of these developments impinged on early childhood music education. The song repertoire widened to include songs from 'other lands', typically songs from the African continent that had lost their connection with a specific country of origin. The emphasis continued – and continues – to be mainly on teaching young children conventional musical basics drawing on a mainly traditional repertoire of children's songs with European roots.

Communities, especially in urban areas, have increasingly diversified in recent years and this has emphasised the importance of all children having equal opportunity, irrespective of race, religion, class, gender or physical ability. Some educators began to point out that inequality was built into systems and institutions and so all aspects of education had to be examined and transformed. It was not enough to merely make surface-level changes to repertoire and curriculum content. There were calls to rethink, at a fundamental level, the underpinning values and priorities in music education with respect for diversities. At the same time, education in general is recognising how all children need to learn to be members of an increasingly diverse and changing society by developing competences such as social awareness, empathy and a sense of justice and fairness.

There have been two areas of research and theorising that have influenced the diversification of music education; ethnomusicology and critical pedagogy. Ethnomusicology has expanded the knowledge base for music education, beyond European traditional music and critical pedagogy has challenged the assumptions that may underlie educational practice.

Ethnomusicology

Ethnomusicologists study all types of musical styles and practices, worldwide, including art musics, folk musics, traditional musics and popular music cultures. They study much more than just the music itself, as musical object, they are interested in how music is a social process that both shapes and is shaped by cultures. They are interested in music as a marker of identity and its many purposes in people's lives. For example, Patricia Shehan Campbell is both an ethnomusicologist and music educator and her studies of children's musical cultures have been interested in how young children use music in their everyday lives for a range of purposes.

Ethnomusicologists are also interested in cultural variations in how music is learned. For example, many musics are not recorded in conventional, European systems of staff notation and so learning them requires aural methods of listen, copy and repeat, or learning systems of chanted pitch and rhythm syllables. As another example, the performance of many musics relies on improvisation and so learning how to improvise is more of a priority than learning how to reproduce and perform music exactly. Understanding different pedagogical approaches highlights the distinctive ways that western art music is learned – with a heavy reliance on staff notation and on exact and accurate reproduction in performance. It also reveals how these conventions have defined practice in methods of early childhood music education.

Inspired by ethnomusicological methods, an interest in children's musical cultures has also grown in recent years (for example, Campbell and Wiggins, 2013). Researchers have studied children's own musical activities and experiences in all kinds of situations and how they participate in musical events. Ethnomusicologists interested in children's playground games, for example, noticed interesting ways that the children learnt from one another by imitating on the sidelines or by joining in as they are able to and gradually become more competent.

Culture Bearer

A culture bearer is a term taken from ethnomusicology. It refers to someone, particularly a migrant, who carries cultural knowledge and values between societies. A culture bearer in music is likely to be someone who has learnt and knows music from a particular culture and can perform it and teach it. The role of culture bearers is valuable in communities where there are many immigrants and diverse cultures coming together. They can make a contribution to educational practice by giving performances and workshops.

Critical Pedagogy

Educators hold positive views of the children and families they work with. However critical pedagogy and the theory behind it suggests that educators may not fully appreciate how society and the institutions of society such as schools create and reproduce social inequalities and give the illusion that those inequalities are natural and fair. When progress and success is thought to be due to individual achievement and not also tied to wider factors in society, these inequalities become embedded in society.

Critical pedagogy tackles these issues and seeks to understand the factors that have resulted in and sustain inequality, in particular racial inequalities, in societies. The approach originated in the USA but has now spread internationally and has developed differently according to the social and cultural contexts of different countries. However, all versions of critical theory share a common understanding of race and racism (or indeed other categories of difference) as a social construct and share a commitment to both understanding and opposing the systems that subjugate people because of their race or other category of difference.

It is important to also recognise that race, gender, class and (dis)ability are all social categories that carry ingrained forms of disadvantage and that these categories operate in concert with one another. This is known as intersectionality.

Culturally Responsive Practices

Culturally responsive practice asks teachers to recognise that how we understand music and music education are influenced by our social identities and our backgrounds. There are two sides to culturally responsive practice; relevance and accessibility:

1. Relevance is increased by taking children's and families' backgrounds and knowledge as a positive learning resource; definitely not as deficits that need to remedied. Building relationships with children and families, knowing about their musical lives, showing respect and understanding, and creating a culture of care come first.
2. With greater relevance comes greater accessibility for the children and families. Teachers understand that it is their responsibility to make the sessions accessible and inclusive, not vice versa.

However, there is a note to add here, that while teachers first need to be able to develop approaches that build on children's and families' existing knowledge, they then also stretch them beyond the familiar, to encourage awareness and sensitivity to diversity.

Words Matter

The terms used to describe music and all that accompanies the music need to be carefully chosen. Terms can have assumptions built into them that we take for granted, but assumptions that may be biased towards certain people. The earlier expression 'music from other lands' then transformed into 'multicultural music education', then gave way to 'intercultural', 'world music' education and teaching music globally. Critical pedagogy recommends that educators should always be quizzing the terms and labels they use to ensure there are no hidden biases and thus to ensure the greatest respect and inclusiveness for people, practices and cultures.

Key Text

Juliet Hess. (2019). *Music Education for Social Change: Constructing an activist music education.* London: Routledge.

Decolonising Music

The core principle of decolonising is to emphasise how colonialism was a central process in creating the modern world. Nate Holder is a leading voice in decolonising the music curriculum in the UK. He points out that colonisation was not only about occupying lands, mistreating indigenous peoples and plundering countries of minerals and crops, but also about imposing beliefs of white superiority. Those who explain decolonising aim to demonstrate how that belief of superiority permeated and continues to permeate every aspect of society including music.

Therefore to decolonise goes much deeper than simply broadening the curriculum to include diverse musics. Superficial approaches to inclusion, diversity and equality do not address the colonial legacy. Conventional music education knowledge is essentially the knowledge of white, middle- and upper-class European men. Women composers, historically, faced many impediments and so their music is much less well known. Black composers likewise. Certain instruments, those of the European symphony orchestra, are thought to be the most valuable for children to learn, and certain types of European classical music are considered to have greatest value for children to listen to. Nate Holder asks music educators to think carefully about what we assume and where we may be turning a blind eye. In short, decolonising asks teachers to look for what and whom has been excluded from the content, repertoire and conceptions of music.

Key Text

Nate Holder. (2020). *Where are All the Black, Female Composers?* London: Holders Hill Publishing.

Representation

All children need to see and hear diverse peoples represented in music and all children need to see themselves and their family reflected positively. In music education, representations of music often depict women, people of other races and with disabilities in limited roles across the spectrum of musical activities. Songs and activities typically assume conventional two-parent families and gender roles.

Representation matters. If children only see white performers and hear white male composers, they come to think that is the norm and what teachers value. If children only see girls playing certain instruments and boys playing other instruments, likewise these norms become rooted in their expectations of what it is to be musical, to be a performer, to be a composer, a conductor, music technology specialist and so on.

Image of Childhood

Diversity approaches in all their different philosophical and theoretical forms are important because they recognise each child as unique and as belonging to particular social and cultural niches. At the same time these theoretical perspectives recognise that race, as with other dimensions of identity, is constructed in multiple different ways in societies. The social construction of childhood in different social groups will always vary, whether the differentiation is by class, ethnic or religious identity.

These theories also challenge us to consider how we may hold preconceived ideas about children of different class, ethnicities and religions or may be inadvertently reinforcing those ideas. For example a romanticised rural childhood is often represented in music activities for young children – songs are about farm animals and being close to nature – and this rural childhood is implicitly white and middle class.

The Theory in Practice

The interaction between ethnomusicology and music education has given rise to a specific approach termed world music pedagogy (WMP). Originating in the USA, the aim of world music pedagogy is to bring a wide range of musical cultures into the consciousness of children with all traditions, styles and genres considered valid. It weaves together active listening, musical participation, performance and creative musical experiences.

In her book *World Music Pedagogy*, Sarah Watts provides a detailed introduction to WMP for early childhood education. The book provides suggestions for repertoire and explains strategies for listening to short pieces of music in focussed ways which are the hallmark of the WMP approach. Listening to and engaging with recorded music is an area of practice that often receives less attention in early childhood music education. The following scenario is inspired by her book.

> A group of 4-year-olds are tired after a long period of outdoor play and are flopping on cushions in the book corner. While they rest the educator plays, at quite low volume, a Chinese recording of Mo Li Hua (Gentle Jasmine) played on a GuZheng (a Chinese plucked zither). She asks the children to lie still and to listen carefully. The children are intrigued by the sound of the instrument, what it looks like and how it might be played. So the teacher then shows a video clip of the GuZheng performance on a wall screen. A few children start to copy the plucking movements of the performer. One child comments that the plucking of strings sounds a bit like the ukulele another teacher sometimes plays. Meanwhile the sound of the music has interested some children playing in another part of the room who come over to listen. The teacher plays the track again and encourages all the children to make 'air plucking' movements as they listen. She asks them to notice and imitate the vibrato effect (that gives the effect of a lengthened note at the end of each phrase). She plays the video clip again so that the children can experience the phrasing again. She tells them the name of the instrument and that it is playing a very old Chinese song. Two children fetch a globe to look for the location of China.

Central to WMP is listening, at increasingly deeper levels. In the activity described above the teacher aimed to:

- encourage attentive listening when the children were relaxed
- encourage engaged listening when the children could watch the performer and imitate his plucking movements, and
- use the enactive experience of pretending to perform the music to emphasise the structure of phrasing.

Combined, these different phases and repeat listenings enabled the children to experience the music from different angles. These learn-to-listen phases are linked to two more phases that include instruction. World music pedagogy sets out the phases thus:

- **Attentive listening** is focused on musical elements and structures. The educator may support the children's listening attentively by directing the children's attention to one part or one feature of the music. The aim is to support the children in listening to the music several times, becoming alert to its features.
- **Engaged listening** involves active participation in some aspect of the music-making (by singing a melody, tapping a rhythm or dancing). Enactive listening encourages a holistic and embodied appreciation of the music, developing children's understanding through another mode.

- **Enactive listening** involves performing the work in some way in which the music is re-created in as stylistically accurate a way as possible. The children may learn to sing a song or play an instrumental part, having come to know the music through attentive and engaged listening. The imitation of a recording – or a live version of the song or instrumental music – is used as the basis of their learning. They learn by ear, trying to recreate the sound and its stylistic characteristics as closely as possible in order to get 'inside' the music.

Later stages of WMP would include the following.

- **Creating world music** in the style of the musical model they have been introduced to. The children may improvise and compose a piece of music that is in the same style and uses some or all of the musical features.
- **Integrating world music** involves a wider introduction to the cultural context of the music that can expand into history, geography, language, literature and the visual and performing arts.

Key Text

Sarah H. Watts. (2018). *World Music Pedagogy, Volume 1: Early childhood education*. New York: Routledge.

Cultural Considerations

Whether working specifically with a WMP approach or more generally being attentive to cultural considerations, teachers engage in a thoughtful process of evaluation of the songs, composers, performers, instruments, books, and curricular materials used and available to children. Questions to ask include the following:

- Whose music/song was it originally? Where is it from and when?
- How did the original music interact with cultural values and practices then and there? How does it interact with values and practices here and now?
- What was the function of the music originally and what is its function now? Has its function changed? – and if so, how?
- How are races, genders, class and age represented in the music and any illustrations that might accompany the pieces of music or songs? Is this representation fair? Does anything reinforce stereotypes of race, gender, or other types of difference?
- Who participates in this music? Who can perform it? How do race, class, gender and age influence who can perform this music and at what times and in what places?
- How is the music performed in its original versions – and where? What kind of physical movement or bodily expression is expected and/or

allowed? Is dancing part of the music? What kind of dancing? Who dances and who maybe does not dance?
- Who is the audience, or is there no audience? Can some people listen and some not? How does the audience engage with the music?
- How is the music passed around – aurally, recordings, internet?
- How is this music learned and from whom? Informally or formally, at home, in the playground, school, church or somewhere else? Is it learnt by ear, or from some kind of notation or recording?
- Does anyone earn money from this music? Is that money fairly distributed?

More specific questions need to be asked about song texts because some songs have questionable lyrics:

- What is the original text? If the song text has been translated, what is the original, exact lyrics and how they should be correctly pronounced?
- What is the song about? What is its meaning and function?
- How are races, genders, class, age and physical ability represented in the song words? Is this representation fair or biased?

A critical pedagogy perspective would ask educators to avoid including songs or music from other cultures:

- as a novelty or exotic addition to the usual, core repertoire. This does nothing challenge the basic belief that certain songs and repertoire are the centre and 'other' songs are marginal and therefore less important. This approach reinforces difference.
- in a trivialised or careless way. A common example is when a song is described as 'a song from Africa' or referring to 'African drumming' without acknowledging that the African continent has over 50 countries and a huge diversity of cultures. This gives the impression that the origins and detail of songs or performance practices are not important and not necessary.
- in a superficial and decontextualised way. The song is introduced without explaining any of the context of the song; whose song is it, when is it sung, for what purpose?
- in a modified form to fit with a particular method or approach. For example, adding an Orff-style accompaniment and changing the rhythms and pitches to fit with the pentatonic scale. Alternatively, by simplifying the rhythms so that young children can use rhythm syllables or distorting the song words in their original language to make them accessible to young children.
- in ways that assume a cultural identity of children based on their family of origin and that overlooks their experiences of growing up in their present community.

Comments and Connections

The assumption that European civilisation represents the most advanced stage of human development and that children's development matches this development was inherent in ideas of recapitulation and primitivism, as we saw in the section that explained these theories. Those ideas in turn underpinned some early-twentieth-century music education methods. These ideas are inherently discriminatory, both in respect of non-European musical cultures and musicians and also in conceptions of very young children as primitive.

Some would argue, however, that social issues concerned with race, gender and so on are not relevant to learning about music. They would say that music can be detached from its social and cultural associations and that there are fundamental skills and core knowledge (the basic elements of music for example) which are common to all music. The focus of music education is to teach these skills and knowledge because they are universal. While it is valuable, they would say, to include a greater variety of songs, music to listen to and musical experiences, music educators do not need to rethink the fundamentals of musical knowledge or the history of Western art music. In other words, music should be judged on inherent aesthetic criteria rather than its social and cultural meanings.

It should be recognised, however, that those who promote critical pedagogy perspectives and work towards culturally responsive and decolonised approaches do not want to do away with the canon of Western art music or the ways of learning music that accompany Western art music, but they want to challenge what they consider to be an inbuilt and assumed superiority. They also point out that a music education focussed only on Western art music practices is narrow and not introducing children to the wide variety of musics in all their richness.

There is another viewpoint which suggests that a focus on diversity has led to an over-simplification of race and that in reality, populations of children are mixed and changing all the time. Children live contemporary lives and we should focus on the present-day realities and not over-emphasise their heritage or dwell too much on a colonial past. They would also argue that economic inequality and class differences have much more significant effects on children's life chances than their race or gender. Tackling these forms of inequality require much more substantial and challenging social and political changes than ensuring non-discriminatory practices with respect to race and gender.

Finally, another criticism is that the calls to ensure diversity and to decolonise music education can have an adverse effect for two reasons. (1) It can result in teachers being so afraid of doing or saying the wrong thing and inadvertently revealing a racist attitude, that they prefer to remain quiet and inactive. (2) While it can be liberating and exciting to include a diversity of musics it can also be overwhelming. A common response is to say that it's not possible to know many types of music and how can teachers teach what they don't know? Others would argue that is an excuse. Doing nothing maintains the status quo. Teachers have to be open-minded, welcome the challenge and be prepared to do the work in educating themselves and look for people, culture bearers, who can help. The parents of children who are being taught can contribute, as can teaching colleagues and other professionals such as artists, community musicians.

Bibliography

Campbell, P. S. (2018) Series foreword. In S. H. Watts, *World Music Pedagogy*, vol. 1, pp. viii–xii. London: Routledge.

Campbell, P. S. and Wiggins, T. (eds). (2013). *The Oxford Handbook of Children's Musical Cultures*. Oxford: Oxford University Press.

Holder, N. and MacGregor, H. (2022). *Listen and Celebrate: Activities to enrich and diversify primary music*. London: HarperCollins.

Lum, C.-H. and Whiteman, P. (eds). (2012). *Musical Childhoods of Asia and the Pacific*. Charlotte, NC: Information Age.

Schippers, H. and Campbell, P. S. (2012). Cultural diversity: Beyond 'Songs from every land'. In G. McPherson and G. Welch (eds), *Oxford Handbook of Music Education*, vol. 1, pp. 87–104. Oxford: Oxford University Press.

Index

Adachi, Mayumi 111
adult-centred 7, 89
Alperson, Ruth 70–1
Andress, Barbara 2, 52–3, 120, 136, 147
Aronoff, Frances 2, 123–27, 166
Art as Experience 40
aural perception 51, 63, 93, 126
aural skills 50, 83 (*see also* inner hearing)

Babysong project 33–4, 154
Bailey, Eunice 2, 55, 58–9, 159
Barnett, Elise Braun 46, 50, 54
Biesta, Gert 3
behaviourism 2, 13, 15, 22–6, 96, 102, 116
Boardman, Eunice 2, 120, 121–23
body percussion 70, 74, 75, 80
Bruner, Jerome 14, 44, 89, 93, 105, 116, 132, 137, 150, 154; influences on music education, 120–25; theory, 117–120
Bruner, J. *The Culture of Education* 119

Cage, John 141, 142
call and response songs 76
Campbell, Patricia Shehan 158–9, 168, 170
Chacksfield, Merle 143–4, 145, 147
child-centred 6–7, 30, 39, 59, 79, 89, 98, 101, 103, 136, 147
children's music 158–9, 170
chronology 12–13
Coleman, Satis 2, 17, 19–21, 141, 143
cognitive development 56, 60, 107, 110, 114, 160; stages of 47, 95–9, 103–4
communicative musicality 129, 149–55, 160

composition, 83, 161; of songs 41–2, 112
concepts of music, 125; formation of 122–3
conservation 100
constructivism 13–4, 39, 53, 79, 96, 107, 113–14, 115, 132, 160, 165
creativity 4, 90, 147, 158; and Froebel, 30, 31–2 41; and Dalcroze, 65, and Orff, 73, 80; and Kodály 88; and play 109, 163; progressive education 157
critical: pedagogy 169–72, 177; theory 171; thinking 26
culture 106–7, 114, 154; bearer 170–1, 178; diversity 6; elite musical 62
cultural psychology 119–20
culturally responsive practice 171–2

Dalcroze eurhythmics 27, 57, 63–69, 72, 85, 103
decolonising 168, 172
Delalande, François 100, 142
democracy 39, 131
Dewey, John 6, 12, 27, 38, 55, 63, 113, 126, 132, 137, 164; philosophy 38–40; philosophy in practice 41–43; principles 40–41
didactic: music materials 52; teaching 25, 89, 165
Dissanayake, Ellen 151
documentation 131, 133–4, 136, 137
Driver, Ann 64; Ethel 64

eco-literate music pedagogy 141–2
elements, musical 35, 44, 65, 103, 162
enactive mode 117–18
enculturation 3, 109
ethnomusicology 20, 79, 129, 139, 141, 158, 169–70, 173

eurhythmics (see Dalcroze eurhythmics)
everyday: music 3, 89, 107, 110, 129, 170; objects 143, 145

folk music 8, 20, 21, 168; Hungarian 81–2, 84–5, 89
Forrai, Katalin 88
Froebel, Friedrich 6, 12, 29, 42–3, 53, 55, 58, 63, 103, 146, 157, 159; and creativity 31;
gifts and occupations, 31; philosophy 30–32;
Froebel, F. *Mother-play and Nursery Songs* 27, 32
Froebel Institute, 29, 58

generative theory of musical learning 121
Gluschankof, Claudia 161
Glynne-Jones, Marjorie 2, 101–2, 126

Hall, Granville Stanley 17–18, 20, 63
Hanna, Wendell 136
Hargreaves, David 99
Holder, Nate 172

iconic mode 117–18, 146
improvisation 90, 161; in Dalcroze 65, 67, 69; in Kodály 83; in Orff 20, 72–4, 76–80, 160
inclusion 172
infant directed: singing 36, 152; speech 36, 152
inner hearing 85
instruments, percussion 31, 75, 83, 96, 142; Orff 75, 79, 90; spontaneous play with 34–5
internalisation 108–9, 117
intersubjectivity 109, 119
Isaacs, Susan 6, 27, 55; principles 56; observation 57–9; holistic development 57, 126

Jaques-Dalcroze, Èmile 6, 12, 20, 54, 62, 63; method in practice, 68–9; philosophy 64–5; principles 65–8; (see also Dalcroze)

kinaesthetic: sense 51, 65; memory 70, 117; music play 161
Kodály, Zoltán 2, 3, 6, 8, 12, 21, 62, 70, 81; method in practice 87–8; philosophy 82–6;

Lancy, David 155
Littleton, Danette 160, 161
lullabies 33, 82

Maccheroni, Anna 46
Malaguzzi, Loris 120, 131–7
Malloch, Stephen 149, 150–51
Malting House School 55, 57
materialism 143
method, music education 8; personalised 8–9
Montessori 6, 12, 27, 46, 63, 70, 137, 146; curve of work 49; and listening 146; music materials 51; philosophy in practice, 50; prepared environment 48; principles 47
Montessori bells 51
motivation, innate 30, 47, 149, 162; and rewards 24
movement: locomotor 50, 66, 70, 74; non-locomotor 66, 74
musical development, models of 101
musique concrète 142
music play: 31–2, 80, 157–58; and Orff 79–80; pedagogy 7, 162, 165; philosophies and theories of, 159; songs and, 31–32; styles of 161 (see also Danette Littleton)
musicianship 6, 61, 64, 81–2, 84

Niland, Amanda 160
notation: 26, 50, 83, 147; graphic 139, 144, 146; reading 44, 61, 63–4, 78; solfa 86; symbolic 96

'operant conditioning' 22
operations 96, 98, 121; pre-operational 100; concrete 97, 100
Orff, Carl 2, 6, 12, 20, 59, 61–2, 72, elemental music 73; pedagogy 77–78, 160; principles 74–6; Schulwerk 72–3; 78
Orff Institute 72

Papoušek, Hanus and Metcheld 151
parents 111, 135, 151, 155; as first educators 39, 49, 154
parenting culture 155
Paynter, John 59, 140, 143
pentatonic scale 84; in Orff, 20, 75–6, 80, 176; in Kodály 84
percussion (see instruments)
Pflederer, Marilyn 100

Piaget, Jean 34, 44, 59–60, 71, 95, 110, 113–14, 126, 137, 142; influences on music education, 99–103; stages of cognitive development 97; sensorimotor explorations 100; theory 96
Pillsbury Foundation School 140
Plowden Report 144
Pond, Donald 158–59
pragmatism 39
prepared environment 48
psychoanalytic pedagogy 55–6, 59, 159

recapitulation 17–21, 68, 79, 125, 159, 177
reflective practice 9
Reggio Emilia 131–38; and Bruner, 116, 120; atelier 134; pedagogy of listening 132, 147; philosophy 135 (*see also* documentation)
rhythm, evolution of music 19–20, 79; foundation of life, 64; of speech 61; sense of 82, 74; syllables 86–7
routines, establishing 24

scaffolding 113, 118, 126–27
schema theory 97, 103, 105
Schaeffer, Pierre 142
Schafer, Murray 141
self-motivated learning 48, 103, 165–6
sensorimotor learning 71, 97, 100–03
Shevock, Dan 141
Sinor, Jean 88, 89
singing: 62; and Froebel, 29, 32; and Eleanor Smith 42; by sight 67, 88; play 113, 162; spontaneous 111; two-part 85 (*see also*, Babysong project)
singing games 70, 82, 87, 161
singing play mats 52
Skinner, Burrhus Frederic 22–4, 106

Smith, Eleanor 27, 38, 41–4, 112
solfa 61, 81, 87, 147; handsigns 85–86; notation 86; tonic 85
solfège 65, 67, 85
Songs for a Little Child's Day 42
social justice 6, 41
sociocultural theory 44, 93, 106, 121, 160
sound exploration 140, 147
soundscape 141
spectrum of song 33
spiral curriculum 119, 121
stages of development: 99, 104, 105, 108; and recapitulation, 18–19; Dewey 40; musical 101; Piaget 60, 96–7; Stanley Hall 20
Stern, Daniel 151
Suzuki method 10
symbolic mode 97, 117–18, 121, 124

The Hundred Languages of Children 132
'time, space, energy' 61
Trevarthen, Colwyn 149–50

'vitality forms' 151
vocal: development 83, 84, 88, 101; range 83, 84
Vygotsky, Lev 44, 96, 105, 106, 126, 132, 137; theory 107; cultural tools 107; and language 108–10; internalisation 108–9; play and creativity 109–12, 160

Watts, Sarah 173
Whiteman, Peter 111
Wiggins, Jackie 111–12
world music pedagogy 173–175

zone of proximal development 108, 113, 118

For Product Safety Concerns and Information please contact our EU
representative GPSR@taylorandfrancis.com
Taylor & Francis Verlag GmbH, Kaufingerstraße 24, 80331 München, Germany

www.ingramcontent.com/pod-product-compliance
Lightning Source LLC
Chambersburg PA
CBHW070316240426
43661CB00057B/2663